FUNDAMENTALS OF CIVIL AND PRIVATE INVESTIGATION

FUNDAMENTALS OF CIVIL AND PRIVATE INVESTIGATION

By

DONALD A. RUSH

Investigation and Security Administrator
Phoenix, Arizona

and

RAYMOND P. SILJANDER

Formerly, Security Investigator and Police Officer
Loss Prevention Engineer
Phoenix, Arizona

CHARLES C THOMAS • PUBLISHER
Springfield • Illinois • U.S.A.

Published and Distributed Throughout the World by

CHARLES C THOMAS • PUBLISHER

2600 South First Street

Springfield, Illinois 62717

© *1984 by* CHARLES C THOMAS • PUBLISHER

ISBN 0-398-04932-7

Library of Congress Catalog Card Number: 83-17903

With THOMAS BOOKS *careful attention is given to all details of manufacturing and
design. It is the Publisher's desire to present books that are satisfactory as to their physical
qualities and artistic possibilities and appropriate for their particular use.* THOMAS
BOOKS *will be true to those laws of quality that assure a good name and good will.*

Printed in the United States of America
Q-R-3

Library of Congress Cataloging in Publication Data

Rush, Donald A.
    Fundamentals of civil and private investigation.

    Includes index.
    1. Detectives — United States. 2. Criminal investiga-
tion — United States. 3. Police patrol — United States —
Surveillance operations.   I. Siljander, Raymond P.   II.
Title.
HV8088.R87   1984   363.2'89   83-17903
ISBN 0-398-04932-7

INTRODUCTION

In preparing this book, the authors have endeavored to cover in one publication a variety of topics of interest specifically to the private investigator. This text covers the fundamental methods and techniques employed by such investigators and is intended to serve as both a learning aid and a source of reference. While certain topics in the book are also covered in books dealing with law enforcement investigations, this text discusses these topics as they apply specifically to investigations conducted outside the realm of law enforcement.

Because the purpose of this book is to discuss the private investigation field in general, a considerable amount of attention has been given to the chapters dealing with *sources of information* and *surveillance*. This was done because of the tremendous importance of these two areas and the frequency with which they are used. The authors have not attempted to include a discussion of all the many specialized applications of private investigations but rather present investigative methods and techniques that are characteristic of virtually all general private investigations.

The authors would like to emphasize the fact that because the topic of this book is private investigations, most of the discussion of techniques and methods is directed at non-law enforcement investigators. These techniques and methods are, therefore, not found in books discussing law enforcement investigations. Law enforcement investigators could, however, benefit greatly were they to utilize some of these techniques. This point is well illustrated by the chapters on "Pretext Investigations" and "Sources of Information." Why stake a place out for hours or days to effect an apprehension when a few pretext phone calls may disclose the subject's whereabouts? Why spend a considerable amount of time interviewing people when it is possible in many cases to obtain the desired information through a few simple pretext phone calls or by examining public records? This publication should be a useful tool not only for private investigators but for law enforcement investigators as well.

Finally, attorneys when preparing their cases have a frequent need for various types of information. Whether an attorney is accustomed to investigating and developing needed information himself or hiring an investigator to develop the information, this book will be an asset as it will make him more aware of where and how to obtain certain types of information, or it may provide him the basis upon which to judge the competence of any investigator whom he may employ.

CONTENTS

FUNDAMENTALS OF CIVIL AND PRIVATE INVESTIGATION

Chapter One

GENERAL ASPECTS

T HIS book deals with the private investigator, whose occupation is essential but frequently misunderstood. The misconception results from the fact that the private investigator tends to operate in a very discreet manner and from the erroneous way in which he is portrayed in movies and on television. Most people already have their own idea of what a private investigator is. Some view him as well tailored and glamorous, while others see him as sleazy and less than reputable. The average private investigator is neither; he is simply an individual who conducts business in a well-informed and methodical manner. Through this text the reader will be shown how, why, and for whom information is gathered and what the private investigator really is.

Initially it would be helpful to define exactly what a private investigator is. *Investigate* means "inquire into, examine thoroughly." That in a nutshell is what a private investigator does. As a matter of fact, that is what any investigator does. What then is a "private" investigator? Simply stated, a private investigator is a person who gathers information and places it into a report form for the benefit of a client or employer. The fact that he works for private individuals or companies is what makes an investigator "private" as opposed to "public," like the investigator who is employed by a governmental organization such as the local police, county sheriff's department, state police, or Federal Bureau of Investigation, to mention only a few of the better-known governmental investigating organizations.

The major differences between the private investigator and the governmental investigator is that the private investigator works for private businesses or individuals. The governmental investigator is generally a sworn law enforcement officer, representing the people, and as such has certain authority that the private investigator does not have. By the same token, however, the governmental investigator operates under certain restrictions that do not apply to the private investigator. The main thing to remember is that the private investigator works for private citizens, whether they are persons or companies.

This basic difference in whom he works for dictates that the type of information the private investigator generally seeks will be different from that generally sought by the governmental investigator. The majority of cases handled by the governmental investigator will someday be tried in a court of law. While it is true that a good many cases handled by private investigators also are tried in a court of law, this is more often the exception rather than the rule.

There are times when a person or company will call on a private investigator to investigate a matter that could have been handled by the police at no charge. The usual reason for not calling in the police is to avoid publicity or to avoid having to prosecute the responsible parties in the event they are discovered. In other instances, private investigators are called upon by clients who are the victims of crimes and wish to have the perpetrators punished, but the local authorities due to understaffing do not have personnel available to follow the cases to their conclusion.

The truly professional private investigator never tries to do the local authorities' job for them. There are times, however, when private investigators and police officers do cooperate on matters that are mutually advantageous. There are no clear-cut guidelines for this mutual cooperation, but it usually comes about on an individual basis and is based on mutual trust and respect. Any good private investigator will always try to cooperate fully with the local authorities. In doing so he will gain their respect, which could in the long run be quite beneficial to him and his clients.

Private investigators and law enforcement officers are not in competition with one another, regardless of what might be portrayed on television and in the movies. On the contrary, the private investigator generally serves those whose investigative needs are such that the local law enforcement agencies have no jurisdiction. Generally speaking, unless an offense has been committed against the state (in other words, unless a crime has been committed), law enforcement agencies are powerless to act. If, for example, someone's spouse had disappeared, and there were reason to believe that foul play was involved, the local law enforcement authorities would conduct an investigation into the matter. However, if it appeared that the missing spouse simply grew tired of the relationship and left, the police would not become involved. It would be necessary, under such circumstances, for the remaining spouse to obtain the services of a private investigator to learn the whereabouts of the missing party, if he or she is unable to do so without help.

There are also some differences in the methods by which police and private investigators work. While governmental and private investigators both utilize interview and surveillance methods extensively, they do so using *variations* of the same basic techniques. Also, governmental investigators utilize physical evidence to a considerable degree, while the private investigator makes extensive use of public and private records and documents. These differences stem from the fact that the governmental investigator is more often concerned with proving that a suspect was at the scene of a crime and building a case for prosecution by way of physical evidence such as footprints, fingerprints, and tool marks. While the private investigator occasionally does this, it is by far the exception rather than the rule.

Simply stated, the primary function of the private investigator is to gather information and write a report for the benefit of a client or employer. It is this ability to gather and report meaningful information that makes the investigator's efforts worthwhile. This ability, then, is what employers or clients are willing to pay for. As in any business or profession, the private investigator will acquire a reputation based on his performance that is either good or bad. That reputation will eventually result in success or failure. Any good private investigator depends upon repeat business from clients and counts on clients to refer new business. Only the investigator who conducts business in a highly ethical and professional fashion will get repeat and referred business. Personal integrity is something that the truly professional investigator must always strive to maintain. In few efforts will personal integrity mean more to eventual success or failure than in the field of private investigation.

PRIVATE INVESTIGATORS AND THEIR EMPLOYERS

Although the sources of information and various means by which it is obtained are numerous, the private investigator will basically employ three methods to acquire desired information for clients. These three methods are *interviews and interrogations*, *record checking*, and *physical surveillance*. This may be somewhat of an oversimplification, but virtually *all* information gathered by private investigators will come from one of these three sources. There are many different applications of these methods; in fact, there are about as many different applications of these methods as there are investigators. For this reason, the discussion of techniques and methods given in this text should serve only as a guideline to the individual private investigator. Each person should apply these methods and techniques in a way that is compatible with his own personality.

Generally speaking, the greatest single user of private investigators is "Big Business." While it is true that many private individuals and small businesses occasionally have need for the services of private investigators, the main employers of these investigators are the large corporations. Those that serve the public, especially, have many areas that occasionally cause problems. Retail stores, for example, are vulnerable to shoplifting, employee stealing, armed robbery, and after-hours burglary, plus a multitude of possible lawsuits resulting from their employee's actions. Any and all of these problems and potential problems can generate business for private investigators.

Usually, the bigger a company is, the more problems it will have, and the greater will be its potential need for the services of a private investigator. However, there are also many relatively small businesses and industrial firms that use investigators quite extensively. Conversely, there are many large firms that seldom use investigators. In other words, any individual or company may at some time or other need to hire a private investigator. The demand for good, competent investigators has grown sharply in the past few years and shows every indication of continuing to grow.

Included among the many large users of investigative services are insurance companies and law firms. Both of these industries have a wide variety of investigative needs. In many cases their investigative needs are satisfied solely by outside investigators, while in other instances these firms have found it advantageous to hire their own investigators to do the bulk of the work and utilize outside investigative agencies to handle the overload work. This practice is not exclusive of the insurance and legal fields, however; many other businesses, because of their large and sometimes unusual needs, also find it beneficial to maintain their own investigative staff.

Because of the growing number of fraudulent claims, the insurance industry has found it increasingly necessary to utilize investigative services to verify the truthfulness of claims. Although insurance companies as a group have been using investigative services for many, many years, individual companies have sometimes felt it cheaper and easier simply to pay a claim rather than incur the expense of having an investigator check it out. Today's rising costs, however, have caused many insurance companies to reevaluate this position. Many companies who had been paying claims without checking them are finding it cost-effective to spend a little money to keep from paying large, fraudulent claims. Insurance companies have always been a good source of business for private investigators, and today's conditions are causing the volume of work from this source to increase.

There are many types of fraudulent claims confronting the insurance claims department; however, the most frequently encountered and quite often the most expensive claims will be for bodily injuries. Many times, when a person is injured in a fall or an automobile accident, for example, the medical profession can neither verify nor disprove the existence of the injury claimed. In cases such as these, insurance companies very often call upon an investigator to conduct a discrete inquiry into the claimant's life-style. The purpose is to determine whether the claimant is behaving in a manner consistent with the nature of the alleged injuries. If, for example, the claimant is allegedly suffering from a "whiplash" injury, one would not expect to find that person out playing tennis. When the insurance company finds out that the claimant is living in a way that is inconsistent with the injuries supposedly suffered, it will usually require that motion pictures be taken of the claimant's activities. With these films the company can usually force the claimant to drop the claim or at least have the settlement greatly reduced. This is just one type of case that will typically prompt an insurance company to request an investigation.

The legal profession, one of the big users of private investigative services, has no single typical type of case that will require the services of an investigator. Attorneys handle an extremely broad range of cases and, therefore, need extremely varied types of information. However, individual attorneys will generally specialize in one or more specific areas of the law.

Although a good investigator can work for almost any kind of employer or client, not every investigator can satisfy the needs of the legal profession without experience in that specific area. The investigator must acquire a basic understanding of legal terminology as well as a familiarity with specific aspects of the legal profession.

PERSONAL QUALITIES AND PROFESSIONAL QUALIFICATIONS

To be truly effective and successful as a private investigator it is necessary to have a complete command of the tools of the trade. This does not mean that an individual must be an expert in all of the many aspects of private investigation, but he must understand the merits and limitations of each aspect of this business and know whom to call upon for assistance when specialized needs arise.

While it is true that the private investigator of today will often take advantage of the inventions that modern science and technology have made available, investigation is still, as it was a thousand years ago, basically an art, not a science. As such it will be an individual's basic ability and resourcefulness that will allow him to operate effectively and efficiently, not his knowledge of science and technology. Technology simply aids the investigator.

The private investigator relies heavily upon his ability to interview and interrogate as well as his ability to cultivate informants. To do these things effectively, the investigator must be the kind of person who is able to meet people easily, place them at ease, and establish rapport with them quickly. Such a person is most often very patient, likable, and resourceful. Such a person must also be persistent, because the desired or necessary informant is not always an easy person with whom to establish rapport.

In some instances it is not possible for the investigator to establish close rapport with a given person. In such cases it is better, as an alternative, to establish rapport with that person's friend in order to achieve the desired results. This is where patience, resourcefulness, persistence, and ingenuity will prove to be great assets to the investigator. The investigator who does not exhibit the basic ability to get along with other people will have little success.

To enhance the basic ability to get along well with others, it is important that the investigator not attract undue attention or cause others to feel antagonistic towards him by his mannerisms or mode of dress. By being more "middle of the road," he will find it easier to get along with people and also will be better able to function without drawing attention to himself. The successful investigator usually trys to be an everyday type of individual who blends in well with everyone.

To be successful, and this is of course what everyone wants to be, the investigator need not be a person of superior intelligence or ability, but he does need to be disciplined and of average intelligence.

The physical health and conditioning of an investigator should not be overlooked. If the investigator is in very poor physical condition, it will be difficult for him to do the job that is required. (Consider, for example, the task of an investigator in poor physical condition faced with conducting a foot surveillance of a subject who is in good physical condition, is a brisk walker, and does not believe in elevators in anything but the tallest of buildings.)

The investigator interested in doing the best possible job will do well to engage frequently in some form of physical activity or sport that will keep his level of physical fitness within acceptable limits. Such things as jogging, swimming, brisk morning or evening walks, and using stairways instead of elevators are all helpful and worthy of consideration.

The investigator who is effective in dealings with people and is able to obtain information from them must also be capable of taking effective and factual notes so that an accurate report can later be prepared, a report that will reflect exactly what the investigator learned in regard to the issue in question. The very basic tools for note taking include a notebook or its equivalent and two pens; the notebook should be a small one that will fit into a pocket and not a large, loose-leaf type that must be carried, and two ball-point pens are necessary since a pen can run dry in the middle of an interview.

In addition to being capable of establishing meaningful rapport with a wide variety of personality types and also being capable of creating intelligible notes and reports, the investigator must be a thorough person who strives to acquire all the facts pertaining to an issue. The investigator who exerts a little extra energy to probe a little more deeply will generally be rewarded for this effort by repeat business from his clients.

The last personal quality that shall be discussed is personal integrity. The private investigator who has all the other necessary qualities but lacks personal integrity will never achieve real success in this business. A client must have the same degree of confidence in a private investigator as in a physician or an attorney. What a client tells the private investigator in confidence must remain in confidence. The truly professional private investigator never discusses a client's business with anyone without first obtaining the client's permission.

Today, almost anywhere in the country that the private investigator chooses to work in, some type of licensing ordinance must be complied with. In some areas, several licenses will be necessary before the investigator can get into business. These licenses come from states, counties, and cities and can vary widely in their requirements. Some localities require only that a small licensing fee be paid and a brief application be placed on file. The license may be granted immediately or after only a brief waiting period. Many licensing agencies require that a bond be posted or a certificate evidencing liability insurance be furnished. Some state licensing agencies require the investigator to furnish statements from references who can verify that he has anywhere from one year's to as many as five year's experience in the business before a license will be granted. This may be coupled with the requirement that he pass a written and/or verbal examination as well. Some states also require that he be a resident of that state for a stated period of time before making application for a license to be a private investigator. In virtually all areas where a license is required to operate, some type of background investigation is conducted on the person making application to determine that he does not have a criminal record.

CASE HISTORY

To illustrate how a *typical* private investigation can develop, the following is an interesting example of a rather extensive investigation conducted for a meat-packing plant on the West Coast of the United States.

The investigation was initially instigated not as a result of suspicion but merely by the client's desire to know the current internal condition of his plant. When reading the case history, the reader will begin to see how several different investigative techniques often work together to bring out the facts of a case.

The initial phase of the investigation involved the placement of an undercover investigator on the client's payroll. By establishing rapport with several employees within the work force the investigator was able to establish the existence of a highly organized theft ring. This ring consisted of a number of loading dock employees including a foreman, order pullers, truck loaders, checkers, and truck drivers. In addition to those directly involved were a number of employees who worked in the area and were being paid to ignore the situation. Subsequent surveillance of the client's trucks revealed they were being overloaded with product, which was being off-loaded at unauthorized stops. In addition, it was learned that entire unauthorized shipments were being scheduled by these employees.

After the accumulation of sufficient evidence, numerous employees were interrogated, and a number of confessions and statements were obtained. Of the sixteen employees directly involved in this incident, six were prosecuted and convicted, with the remaining ten being terminated. The cost of the investigation to the client was small when compared to the loss of $600,000 in products that was incurred over a six-month period of time.

Chapter Two

REPORT WRITING

I T has been said that an investigator is only as good as his sources of information. It can also be said that an investigator is only as good as the reports that he writes. Many otherwise good investigators experience a considerable degree of difficulty with this most necessary function. If an investigator does an outstanding job of developing information while in the field but is unable to convey his findings in a written report that is clear and concise, he will be of limited value to a client or employer. For such an individual to be of any value, it would be necessary for someone to write his reports for him. This cannot be, for one supervisor faced with the task of writing reports for several investigators working under his direction would have little time for anything else.

When someone pays a fee for investigative services, whether it be to an outside agency or to his own in-house investigators, he is not paying for the investigation so much as he is paying for the resulting report and the information it reflects. The report is actually the product, whereas the investigative skills and methods used to obtain the information in the report are simply the tradesman's tools by which the investigator creates the final salable product. The client is generally interested in the contents of a report, not how they were obtained.

When preparing a report, the investigator should not attempt to impress its readers by using terminology that is characteristic of the trade. Such terminology is acceptable only in the event that the reader is himself an investigator. Reports should be prepared using layman's terminology so that they can be easily and properly interpreted by the reader. It should go without saying that a written report is a *must* regardless of whether or not a verbal report is made. Furthermore, if a report is to be of value, it must be promptly prepared and forwarded to the requesting party.

When it becomes necessary to provide a physical description of a person in a report, the description should be presented in the generally accepted format that is as follows:

1. Sex
2. Color
3. Age
4. Height
5. Weight
6. Build
7. Complexion
8. Hair
9. Eyes
10. Peculiarities
11. Dress

Example: Male, Caucasian, 25 years old, 5 feet 9 inches, 150 pounds, average build, medium complexion, brown hair, blue eyes, heavy sideburns, walks with slight limp, wearing jeans, long-sleeved tan shirt, brown socks, and black shoes

When describing a vehicle, the following format may be used:

1. Year
2. Color (top over bottom)
3. Make
4. Model
5. Year of registration
6. State of registration issue
7. Registration number

Example: 1975, white over red, Ford Pinto, two-door sedan, 1976 Arizona registration number RPD-643

There are not only a number of types of reports that investigators will create, depending upon the type of investigation conducted, there are also a variety of formats that will be required, depending upon by whom the investigator is employed. Some type of identifying heading should be put on all but undercover reports. (The headings of undercover reports should include only the date and investigator's number or some other identifying symbol.) Generally speaking, all other reports should have a heading that includes the name of the person or company requesting the information, the date, an identifying file number, the investigator's name or initials, and/or the investigative agency's name. How these items are actually set forth on the report is not important.

Following is an example of a typical background investigation report employing a narrative style with source captions:

NO NAME DETECTIVE AGENCY

Report Prepared for:
ABC Manufacturing Company
File number: X743
Background Investigation

Commenced: 9:00 am

Date: June 7, 1984

Investigator: TMB
Subject: John J. Smith

Discontinued: 5:00 pm

CRIMINAL

Superior Court Records
Criminal Division
Maricopa County
Phoenix, Arizona

Criminal records from January 1, 1972 to present in the name John J. Smith were searched. Several files were reviewed because of the common name, but all were determined to be someone other than the subject in question.

CIVIL

Superior Court Records
Civil Division
Maricopa County
Phoenix, Arizona

Civil records were searched from January 1, 1972 to present, and the following action was found:

Date: September 12, 1978
File No.: C-19876
Plaintiff: Lewis Oil Company
Defendant: John J. Smith
Nature of Action: Suit for monies due
Disposition: Judgement for plaintiff, $1,200 plus court costs and attorney fees.

DIVORCE

Superior Court Records
Divorce Division
Maricopa County
Phoenix, Arizona

Divorce records were searched for John J. Smith, and no action was found for Smith either as plaintiff or as defendant

EMPLOYMENTS

Acme Trucking Company
1045 N. 14th Street
Phoenix, Arizona
Sam Brown, Dispatcher

Mr. Brown was contacted under a suitable pretext and stated that John J. Smith has worked for Acme since December 6, 1979 as a truck driver. He

is currently working as a long-haul
driver and has a good work record.

Red's Trucking Company
3056 W. 19th Avenue
Phoenix, Arizona

Mr. Wilson stated that John J. Smith
was employed by Red's Trucking Company from December 6, 1973 to No-
vember 4, 1979. He was terminated by
the company due to a fight he was involved in with another employee. His
work record was good up to that point,
but he would not be considered eligible
for reemployment.

NEIGHBORHOOD

798 W. Central
Phoenix, Arizona

This is a single-family dwelling located in an average, middle-class, residential area. The Smith home is estimated to be worth $58,000 and
compares favorably with others in the
neighborhood.

Neighbors contacted in this area
stated that the Smiths have lived here for
about seven to eight years. They are
buying their home. Mr. Smith is known
to be a truck driver for a local firm, but
Mrs. Smith is not employed. The Smiths
are known to be good neighbors and
cause no trouble. In the past, shortly after they moved in, Mr. Smith had been
known to come home in an intoxicated
condition periodically, and they had considerable financial difficulties, as bill
collectors frequented their home.
Neighbors state they have not seen any
bill collectors or Mr. Smith in an intoxicated condition for several years.
Nothing further of a derogatory nature
was learned about either Mr. or Mrs.
Smith.

In a background investigation report, the actual layout or sequence of information is not important. The report must simply be easy to read and interpret.

The following is a sample of a narrative-style, time-captioned surveillance
report:

NO NAME DETECTIVE AGENCY

Report Prepared for: *Date:* June 8, 1984
File Number: X-744   *Investigator:* PDQ
Surveillance

Commenced: 3:00 am   *Discontinued:* 12:30 pm

3:30 am: I arrived in the vicinity of the XYZ Trucking Company yard and 5657 W. 5th Avenue, Los Angeles, California.

3:37 am: I observed a truck described as "Ford Tractor with Strick Trailer, Cab Unit #347, Trailer Unit #117, Cab License #30409, Trailer License #RL2345," pulling out of the yard. I began surveillance of the truck at this time.

4:42 am: The truck arrived at Sophie's Market, 4219 E. Polk Avenue, Canoga Park, California. Due to the position of the truck and lack of available concealment, I was unable to count the number of baskets delivered to this store. The truck was then observed leaving and being driven across the street to the Green Door Market, 32011 Herman Boulevard, Canoga Park, at 5:20 am. Again the same conditions existed as in the previous stop, and I was unable to take a count. The truck departed at 6:00 am.

6:30 am: The truck arrived at Fred's Ranch Market, 2069 San Jose Road, Burbank, California. The driver delivered sixty (60) baskets of eggs to this store and picked up twenty (20) empty baskets, before leaving at 7:10 am.

8:00 am: The truck was observed stopping behind Sam's Market, 2532 Madison Way, Culver City, California. The driver delivered thirty (30) baskets of eggs, picked up forty (40) empty baskets, and left at 8:27 am.

8:50 am: The truck arrived at the White Market, 1269-149th Street, Torrance, California. A delivery of one hundred seventy-five (175) baskets was observed by this investigator; thirty (30) empties were picked up, and the truck was driven away at 9:50 am.

10:02 am: Subject truck was observed to stop on the side of the roadway in the 2000 block of North 3rd Street, Gardena, California. At this time a vehicle described as "1974 Chevrolet pickup truck, blue, with California registration BK 9432" pulled up behind the subject truck, and the drivers of both vehicles engaged in a brief conversation between the vehicles. They then proceeded to open the subject truck and remove twenty-five (25) baskets of eggs, which were placed in the pickup truck. Both drivers then returned to their respective vehicles and departed the area at 10:17 am.

11:15 am: The subject truck was observed being driven into the XYZ Trucking Company yard at this time. I discontinued the surveillance and returned to Los Angeles to write this report.

In the interest of professionalizing their reports, many investigators have elected to include a synopsis or summary at the beginning. The synopsis/summary is a brief statement generalizing the information contained within the body of the report and can be a great help to a busy client, especially if the investigator is submitting a high volume of written reports to him. The synopsis/summary should tell the client whether it is a favorable or unfavorable report and may include a recommendation or an opinion if the client has asked for such comments.

Chapter Three

INTERVIEWS, INTERROGATIONS, AND STATEMENTS

O NE of the methods of gathering information most widely used by investigative personnel, regardless of what phase of investigative work they are engaged in, whether it be law enforcement or private investigation, is interviewing people. It is not uncommon for an investigator, perhaps several investigators, to spend days interviewing people in connection with one particular case. The days can, in some cases and not infrequently, extend into weeks and perhaps even months.

On the surface, the interviewing of people appears to be an easy task that requires little qualification on the part of the investigator. On the contrary, however, interviews must be carefully planned and the people carefully approached if successful results are to be realized. Prior to conducting interviews, the investigator must fully familiarize himself with every aspect of the case and exactly what it is he intends to learn. It is important that some prior thought be given to who is to be interviewed, what information each person may be in possession of, and what the most logical and productive order in which to approach the people is. The importance of this point can best be illustrated by considering willing and hostile witnesses and those people who do and do not have a vested interest in the outcome of the case. In all cases, hostile witnesses should be interviewed last, as they are most likely to lie and attempt to misrepresent an issue. The more factual information the investigator has in his possession when he interviews these people, the less chance there will be that they will be successful in confusing or misleading him. People with an interest in the case will often provide information in the manner best suited to their interests.

Interviewing can be distinguished from interrogating in that interviews are generally done in a relaxed manner and without any form of accusation being made. The interviewer usually seeks the freely given testimony of various people, whereas an interrogation generally focuses on a *suspect* during the accusatory stage of an investigation.

When conducting an interview, the investigator will either do so openly and without any pretext or will do so in an undercover manner using a fictitious name and reason for requesting the desired information. An example of the latter is seeking certain information about an individual by contacting his neighbors under the guise of updating the party's insurance or contacting an individual's family or friend and requesting his whereabouts under the pretext that the investigator is a casual aquaintance who owes the party a modest sum of money.

INTERROGATION

As stated earlier the interrogation is most often conducted in the accusatory stage of an investigation. Unlike the people who are interviewed, the people interrogated are generally suspect.

Often, the investigator conducting an interrogation has substantial information with which to work, such as actually knowing that the person being interrogated committed a given act, and is simply trying to obtain a confession and subsequently a statement to support whatever evidence is already in his possession. In other instances, the investigator only suspects the individual of having committed some particular act or possess some knowledge of it and is playing on a lead or "shooting in the dark."

The reader should understand that the procedure commonly referred to as "interrogation" is not actually so much an interrogation as it is an interview or question-and-answer session. In virtually all cases where the private investigator is conducting an "interrogation," he is doing so with the subject's tacit approval. The private investigator must understand that he has no power or authority by which to compel the subject to stay for the interrogation; the subject may leave at any time he desires.

Qualifications of the Interrogator

Interrogation is an art in that not just anyone can master it. Many practitioners have come to refer to it as a game of "psychological chess," inasmuch as it is often a match of wits between the interrogator and his subject. While many investigators conduct interrogations on a regular basis, a large percentage of them never become highly skilled and successful at it.

Even though few investigators will ever become true masters of interrogation, they can, with a bit of forethought, preparation, and training, become reasonably competent. An important step toward becoming a good interrogator is for the investigator to assist and observe a skilled interrogator at work before attempting to conduct an interrogation himself. Following is a list of traits that have proven over the years to be desirable characteristics for an interrogator to possess. It should be understood, however, that no one interrogator will possess all of these qualities.

1. *Capable of commanding respect:* The interrogator must be able to maintain control at all times over the subject of the interrogation. This must be accomplished through the force of the investigator's personality.
2. *Sincerity and integrity:* The subject must believe in the sincerity and integrity of the interrogator before he will relate to him.
3. *Perseverance:* This quality is essential, especially in cases of uncooperative subjects or seemingly cooperative subjects whom the interrogator has reason to believe may be withholding information.
4. *Sound logic:* The course of questioning must be conducted in an orderly and logical manner so that the interrogation process will move steadily toward the ultimate objectives set for the interrogation.
5. *Self-control:* The interrogator must guard against losing his temper or allowing the subject to confuse or mislead him.
6. *Observation and interpretation:* The interrogator must have the ability to observe and interpret correctly the subject's actions and reactions. The interrogator must be capable of altering his strategy according to the manner in which the subject is responding to his questions.

Physiological Cues

There are a number of physiological indicators that a trained interrogator should be alert for. While these indicators can be helpful when properly interpreted, they are not absolute signs of innocence or guilt. The following indicators, when viewed in light of the subject's temperament, can provide valuable insight to the skilled interrogator and thus assist him in properly altering his course of questioning in accordance with the subject's reactions:

1. Sweating
2. Dry mouth
3. Rapid pulse
4. Color changes
5. Breathing

Planning and Conducting the Interrogation

In most cases the interrogation is being conducted as a result of information that has been developed through other investigative procedures, such as surveillance or undercover operation. This being the case, the investigator conducting the interrogation will generally have some information with which to work. In preparing for and conducting an interrogation the investigator must consider a number of things, depending upon the circumstances under which the interrogation will be conducted:

1. Adequate space is necessary.
2. Anything that may cause a distraction should be removed.
3. Two (2) interrogators should be employed if possible (always in the event a female is to be interrogated).
4. If the interrogation is conducted in regard to employee infractions, the subject's employer should not be present in the room; however, he should be available to answer questions concerning company policy should they arise.
5. Should a union employee be the subject of an interrogation, any request for the presence of a union representative must be honored.
6. Interrogation of a company employee should be conducted during that person's normal working hours, and he must be paid for the time spent in the interrogation room. Accordingly, he must comply with his employer's instructions to meet with the interrogators; however, he need not make a statement.
7. When conducting successive interrogations of employees within a company, adequate space is necessary to hold the employees, after they have been questioned, separate from the other employees yet to be questioned.
8. When questioning employees regarding information obtained through an undercover investigation while the undercover investigator is still operating within the company, it is usually desirable to question the undercover investigator along with the other employees. When this is the case, the undercover investigator should be questioned early in the interrogation process so that he can be placed into the holding area to monitor anything the employees already interrogated may discuss. Many times this brings out additional information that might not otherwise have been obtained.
9. After the initial interrogation has been completed, it is often desirable to reinterrogate the undercover investigator along with other employees, in order to learn what has been discussed in the holding area. This information, along with other information learned during the initial interrogation process, can provide the basis for further questioning of key suspects.
10. During the interrogation, it is important that adequate notes be taken at all times. The investigators conducting the interrogation must be prepared to take a statement promptly should a witness be agreeable to providing one or in the event a suspect offers a confession.

STATEMENTS

In preparing a written statement, the investigator should be aware of and observe a few basics to insure the statement's acceptance in a court of law. These basics are as follows:

1. It is desirable to have the statement made in the subject's own handwriting.
2. Lines should not be skipped or blank spaces left when preparing the statement.
3. The statement should be written from one edge of the paper to the other, leaving no border.
4. Terminology which is consistent with that used by the subject should be used. This should not present a problem if the subject writes the statement himself.
5. If the statement is not prepared in the subject's own handwriting, a couple of obvious errors should be included so that he may correct them in his own handwriting. The corrections should then be initialed by both the subject and the investigator.
6. The subject and the investigator should sign each page at the bottom.
7. One (1) side of the paper only should be written on, the back side should have a line drawn through it.

The following is a typical statement. Although there are many differing formats, the information reflected in this sample is characteristic of statements in general.

STATEMENT

Statement of ____(subject name)____ made to ____(investigator)____ at ____(address)____ , on the __(date)__ day of __(month)__ , 19 _(year)_ , at _(time)_ o'clock _(a or p)_m.
I have been advised that I need make no statement unless I desire to do so, anything I may say can be used against me in a criminal action. I am _(age)_ years of age, ____(married, single, etc.)____ , live ____(alone, wife, number of children)____ at ____(residence address)____ , and am employed as a ____(occupation)____ by ____(employer)____ at __(business address)__ .

(Body of Statement)

I have read the foregoing statement, consisting of ___(number)___ pages, and I state that it is all true. This admission is made voluntarily, without restraint, coercion, or by virtue of any promise of any kind. I have received a copy of this statement.

Signed _____(subject's signature)_____

The foregoing was signed in my presence by ___(print subject's name)___, who declared that he had carefully read it, that the contents were thoroughly understood, and that each statement therein was true.

Witness ___(signature and date)___   Witness ___(signature and date)___

POLYGRAPH
AND PSYCHOLOGICAL STRESS EVALUATOR

Polygraph

The polygraph, often referred to as a "lie detector," is considered by many to be a useful tool when utilized in conjunction with other investigative techniques. Because of the many variable characteristics connected with the use of the polygraph, the investigator should not rely on its results exclusively; since the results of the polygraph are based on both how the subject interprets questions asked by the examiner and how the examiner interprets the subject's reactions to his questions, the findings cannot be considered absolute. Many states actually prohibit the use of polygraph examinations as a condition of employment or continued employment; however, when properly employed, the polygraph has proven to be a most useful aid. Before the investigator endeavors to utilize the polygraph, he should be aware of any laws regulating its use in the state in which he intends to operate.

Psychological Stress Evaluator

The Psychological Stress Evaluator or PSE performs basically the same service as does the polygraph; however, it does so by a different method. Unlike the polygraph, which measures physiological changes through the use of body attachments, PSE accomplishes this task solely by detecting stress in the human voice. As with the polygraph, PSE should be used only as a supplementary aid to other investigative techniques.

Chapter Four

PHYSICAL SURVEILLANCE

INTRODUCTION

EARLIER it was stated that while conducting an investigation, the investigator will frequently obtain information by using interview and interrogation techniques and by examining various public and private records and documents. In many instances, however, the needed information is not obtainable through such techniques or sources, and he must determine if it can be obtained by watching directly activity that may be of significance. Accomplishing this may involve observing activity at a given location (*stationary surveillance*) or following a person as he moves about the community (*moving surveillance*).

Watching and following people and vehicles is referred to as *physical surveillance*. The investigator conducting a surveillance is often referred to as the *surveillant*, while the person being observed is referred to as the *subject*.

This chapter introduces the various methods and techniques of physical surveillance. An examination will be made of methods and techniques of stationary surveillance, foot surveillance, and vehicle surveillance. Each technique will be discussed in sufficient detail to enable the reader to make a valid judgment as to when it is appropriate.*

Using proper techniques at proper times is important. Failing to do so can result, in some instances, in unnecessarily high costs in terms of work hours, and it can also result in an unsuccessful investigation. Because of the variety of conditions under which surveillances are conducted, and because the needs of each case will differ, the investigator should try to use variations of these techniques as conditions warrant.

Making quick decisions in the field requires both experience and a good understanding of basic surveillance techniques. Making good decisions also requires having confidence in one's ability to do so effectively. Generally, confidence comes as a result of competence, and competence comes only as a

---

*For a more extensive discussion, see Siljander, Raymond P.: *Fundamentals of Physical Surveillance.* Springfield, Charles C Thomas Publisher, 1978.

23

result of diligent study followed by practice in the field. Frequent practice is very important, and the inexperienced should obtain it even if it means randomly selecting people on the street and following them.

Because a physical surveillance is so often conducted only when other investigative methods have failed to produce the needed information, proficiency in this art is essential. When a surveillance is conducted as a last resort effort, the ultimate success of the case can rest on the success of the surveillance operation.

It is often thought that when conducting a surveillance the main goal is staying with the subject while avoiding detection; however, the main goal is observing everything that may pertain to the matter being investigated. Staying with the subject and avoiding detection is only the means by which the real objective is achieved. It is important, therefore, that the investigator possess good powers of observation and the ability to remember what he observed. He must also be able to prepare a report that clearly reflects his observations.

REASONS FOR SURVEILLANCE

The reasons for conducting a physical surveillance depend upon the specific needs of a case, but all the various reasons consistently lead back to one basic objective: gathering information. The nature of the information will depend upon the specific needs in question. The following list, by no means complete, provides some typical reasons for conducting a physical surveillance:

1. To obtain information or develop leads
2. To obtain evidence of a crime that has been committed
3. To observe a crime or irregularity actually being committed
4. To check the reliability of informants
5. To check the loyalty of employees
6. To determine if a subject is frequenting a certain location
7. To determine a subject's habits
8. To observe meetings and transactions
9. To determine when and where an individual will be available for the serving of papers
10. To determine an individual's availability for an interview, interrogation, or apprehension
11. To establish or verify the identity of a subject or the subject's contacts
12. To obtain photographs (useful in many cases, such as sale of contraband, theft, and fraudulent disability claims)

SURVEILLANCE AIDS

In addition to understanding the various surveillance methods and techniques and being reasonably proficient in their use, the investigator must also be familiar with the various optical tools used to extend the effectiveness of vision under various conditions, such as during daylight hours and at night.

The use of visual aids is important because a physical surveillance is conducted for the purpose of making *visual* observations. The operation will be most productive only if the investigator making the observations does so efficiently. Investigators who neglect to use such equipment soon discover that they are severely limited by distance and by low-light conditions.

Once in a position to effectively observe a subject or location, the investigator will many times wish to make a visual record of observations. Thus it is necessary to know how to use a camera, both still and motion picture. Because of the importance of being able to use surveillance aids properly, additional material will be devoted to this topic later.

Another tool made available through radio technology is the electronic locating and tracking system, often referred to simply as the *bumper beeper*. This system consists of a miniature radio transmitter that emits either a continuous or pulsating radio signal. The transmitter is usually concealed on.the undercarriage of a subject's vehicle, which the investigator will later attempt to locate and/or follow. Mounted in the investigator's vehicle is a special radio receiver that picks up the incoming signal and indicates the approximate direction and distance of the subject's vehicle in relation to the investigator's vehicle.

Certain legal restrictions placed upon the use of this equipment are discussed in greater detail in the chapter on legal constraints. No investigator should attempt to use this or any other piece of electronic equipment without fully understanding the laws pertaining to its use.

STATIONARY SURVEILLANCE

Preparing for a Stationary Surveillance

Almost any surveillance operation will require stationary surveillance at some point. Some cases require an operation that consists entirely of stationary surveillance; the activity occurring at a given location is observed and/or photographed, but no one is followed. In the case of moving surveillance, a stationary surveillance technique will almost always be employed while the investigator waits for the subject to leave an area.

It is important that a preliminary survey be made of the area in which the surveillance is to occur, so that a good *vantage point* can be selected. The vantage point is the location from which observations will be made. A great deal of care must be exercised when selecting a vantage point, with the degree of care becoming increasingly important the longer the operation is expected to last. Although some stationary surveillance operations have been known to continue for a year or more, this is unusual. Private investigators generally find that surveillance lasting a few days to a week or more is considered fairly long-term.

When selecting a vantage point, many factors must be taken into consideration, the most important consideration being that the vantage point offer an unobstructed view of the area of interest while at the same time providing sufficient cover or concealment so that the subject of the surveillance does not become aware of the operation. In some instances, the subject, upon seeing the investigator, may not realize that he or she is being surveilled but may become curious or suspicious. This is not desirable.

In many instances, no single vantage point will offer a view of the area that is entirely unobstructed, meaning that from one point it is possible to see part of the area of interest, with the remaining area being visible only from another location. When this situation exists, the investigator must decide if the importance of the case will justify the cost of two or more investigators, so that each can surveil a portion of the subject area. If this can be done, little problem exists. If more investigators cannot be assigned to the case, however, then a determination must be made regarding which area is most likely to reveal the desired activity. Often nothing more than an educated guess can be made, and it will not be until after some activity has occurred that a good position can be achieved. Another disadvantage is that once activity has occurred and an appropriate change of the vantage point is made, later activity can be of a different nature and occur at a location that is again out of the investigator's view.

A good example of this occurred in a fairly typical, actual case. In Figure 4-1 is depicted a parking lot that was used as a vantage point by investigators to surveil a house on the opposite side of the street. On almost a daily basis, at almost the same time each day, a truck would stop at the residence across the street from the parking lot. On some days the driver would park close to the house and steal a portion of product from the truck by transferring it into the house to be picked up after work. This activity was visible to some degree to the investigator parked in position A in the parking lot.

On other occasions, however, the driver would park next to the shed and siphon large quantities of gas from the truck. This could be observed and photographed from position B in the parking lot. When the investigators were occupying position A, it was not possible to observe the activity visible from position B because the delivery truck obstructed the view. Similarly, it was impossible to see, from position B, the activity that was visible from position A, because, again, the delivery truck obstructed the view. From either the A position or the B position, only some activity was visible, with the truck blocking the view of the other. Never knowing which activity would be occurring next, the investigator could not know which vantage point to utilize.

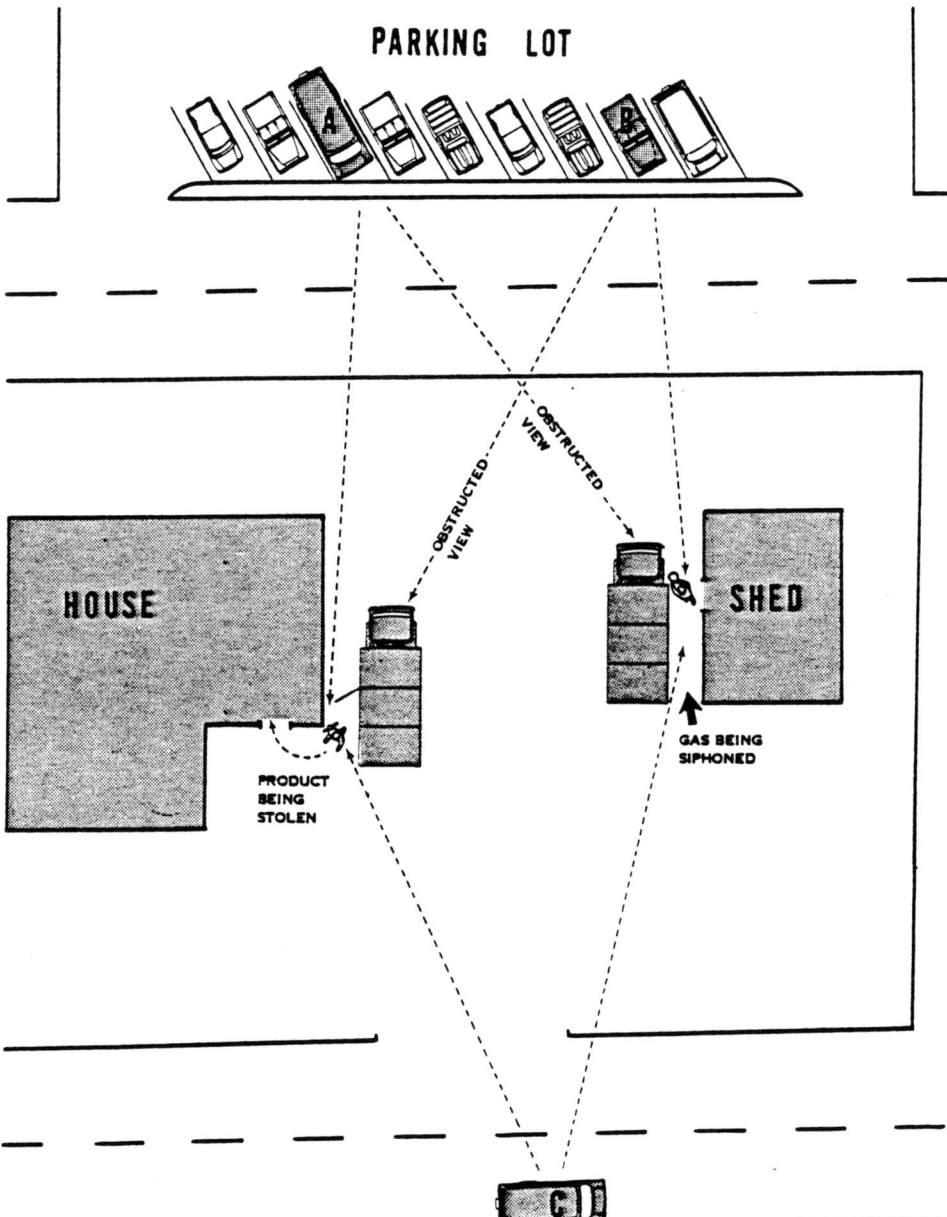

Figure 4-1. Often no single vantage point will afford an unobstructed view of the entire area of interest. Positions A and B offer good concealment but limited visual coverage. Position C, while more vulnerable to detection by the subject, offers good visual coverage.

In this particular case it was decided that a greater loss was occurring as a result of stolen product being removed into the house. For this reason, position A was selected as the most desirable. On a few occasions it was desirable and possible to discreetly move to position B, while the driver was in the house. Although position A enabled the investigator to observe and photograph the fact that unloading of product was taking place, the truck's door in the open position greatly restricted the investigator's view, enough so that it was impossible to effectively document photographically precisely *what* and *how much* was being stolen.

After three days of working from positions A and B, it was decided that any additional time spent at those two locations would result in further evidence of the same nature but nothing new or better. It was then that a surveillance truck was parked in the street at position C on the opposite side of the house. Although this position offered a much better view of the activity of interest, it was decided to work from that position last because the nature of the neighborhood was such (residential, but vehicles *rarely* parked in the street) that a vehicle parked on that street could attract unwanted attention, especially if left there for an extended period of time.

By using what was learned from the first three days of the surveillance, it was possible, with one investigator secreted in the truck, for a second investigator to drive the vehicle into position, park it, and walk away. This was done not more than thirty minutes prior to the subject's expected arrival, and the truck was removed shortly after the subject left the area. The vehicle was not removed so soon, however, as to make it obvious that its arrival and departure were in any way related to that of the subject. To allay the subject's suspicion, "Lawn Care" service signs were placed on the sides of the vehicle, thus giving it an appearance of belonging.

Had an attempt been made to work from position C initially, the desired evidence might have been obtained the first day. However, if something had gone wrong and the subject had become alerted, it is highly possible that the evidence might have been lost altogether. By initially working from positions A and B, both of which offered a less desirable view but much better cover and *then* working from position C, if something did go wrong at the latter location, the investigators still had the benefit of that information which had been previously obtained from a safe location.

Two things should be evident from this example. First, if no single vantage point that offers an unobstructed view of the area is available, an effort should be made to select the one that offers the *greatest* likelihood of success. Second, if some vantage points offer ideal cover but a limited view of the area while others offer an excellent view but limited cover, the investigator must consider the merits of each along with the inherent risks. In the example given, position C worked out well. Had it been tried on the first day, however, and failed, it might very well have meant an unsuccessful investigation.

When planning for stationary surveillance, the position of the sun in relation to the subject's position and the investigator's is an important consideration, especially when photographing is to occur. The most desirable situation is that with *side lighting,* with the sun just slightly ahead of the subject. *Front lighting* is second best with *back lighting* being very undesirable.

The reason side lighting is preferable to front lighting is that side lighting tends to create enough shadow to bring out depth and detail. Front lighting has a tendency to offer a flat, washed-out appearance. Back lighting causes a silhouette. Every effort should thus be made to select a vantage point that offers side or front lighting.

The expected time period of the surveillance is a relevant consideration. If the investigator is beginning a surveillance in the morning with the sun to his back, toward afternoon the sun will have moved, thus providing first overhead lighting and finally back lighting. In some cases, the vantage point can be changed in the afternoon. In other instances, the investigator will be forced to observe as well as possible with back lighting.

It was previously stated that when conducting moving surveillance, the investigator must be familiar with stationary surveillance techniques, since generally stationary surveillance is necessary while waiting for the subject to leave an area. When selecting a vantage point for moving surveillance, the investigator must consider all possible directions and avenues by which the subject may leave the area and the appropriate course of action in each instance. This is important because in many moving surveillances, if the subject is lost, it is within the first few blocks, because of poor planning and positioning on the part of the investigator.

A knowledge of stationary surveillance techniques is important also when conducting moving surveillance because when the subject reaches a destination, the investigator will generally utilize a stationary technique to observe his subsequent activity.

During the preliminary survey, the investigator should make mental notes as to the type of vehicle and mode of dress appropriate for the locale to be able to blend with the environment and appear to belong when conducting the surveillance. By this is meant that someone conducting the surveillance in an upper middle class neighborhood should dress in a manner consistent with others in that neighborhood and drive a reasonably new and well-kept vehicle. However, should the surveillance take place in a commercial or warehouse district, the same vehicle and mode of dress may not appear natural.

When conducting the preliminary survey, the investigator should make an effort to accomplish the task in a very discreet manner so that his presence and activity do not become apparent to others in the area. Exactly how best to accomplish this will depend upon the area and the requirements of the investigation. In some instances, the only reasonable method will be to drive through the area, but the investigator should avoid driving through repeatedly. If it is necessary to make several passes, a change of vehicles is desirable. In other instances, the investigator can walk or ride a public conveyance through an area.

In some instances a combination of these methods may be in order, or the investigator may find that a detailed study of the area can be made from a distance, with or without the aid of optical equipment such as binoculars or a telescope. When dealing with a rural setting, it may prove advantageous to fly over the area and possibly even take a few aerial photographs for planning purposes. Aerial photographs of an urban area can generally be obtained from the city engineer's office, also.

Last, but by no means of least importance, is the need to determine the time period in which the surveillance should be conducted. This consideration is very important because to attempt the surveillance during a period of time that is not likely to produce the desired results is costly in terms of work hours, and there is an increased likelihood that the operation will be discovered. It should be remembered that the longer a surveillance is conducted, the more difficult it becomes to maintain a *covert* operation.

Automobiles and trucks, rooms within nearby buildings, rooftops, and outdoor observation posts can all be used as bases for stationary surveillance. These all have good and bad features, even though some are inherently better than others.

Automobiles as Observation Posts

Automobiles are a means of transportation, a means by which people travel from one location to another. Once at the desired location, people do not normally sit in their vehicle but rather get out and walk away. This is why automobiles are not ideal for use as observation posts. Anyone sitting in an automobile for prolonged periods of time is subject to scrutiny and suspicion by people in the area, and often a report will be made to the local police, who will most likely investigate the complaint.

Despite the shortcomings of the automobile as an observation post, however, it is used a great deal for such purposes. An automobile can be necessary when the surveillance will result in an apprehension and/or pursuit or when the surveillance is for the purpose of following a subject's vehicle when it leaves the area. In other instances, the automobile is used for lack of anything better under the circumstances.

When the investigator must use an automobile for an observation post, every effort should be made to position the vehicle so that its presence is not conspicuous. Parking among other parked vehicles, for example, such as in a parking lot or along a street offering on-street parking generally provides good cover. When utilizing other vehicles for cover, however, the investigator should park in a manner consistent with them, for to do otherwise can make his vehicle *very* conspicuous. For example, if the parking lot has painted lines to regulate the placement of parked vehicles, he should not park in violation.

When parking on a public street, an effort should be made to watch from the next block, because a vehicle on the same block is more likely to be noticed. *Never* should the investigator park directly in front of or across the street from the subject's location. If circumstances require him to do so, a van or camper should be used. When working from the next block, binoculars are often necessary to make meaningful observations and to read vehicle registration numbers. Parking on the next block is desirable also from the standpoint that in the event people in the immediate vicinity do become aware of the surveillant's activity, the subject will remain unaware.

When the investigator cannot avoid parking the vehicle in a location that is closer to the subject's position than is felt safe, he should consider positioning the vehicle so that it is facing the other way and observing the subject through the rearview mirror. While observing in that manner is naturally not as good as watching something directly, it is better than alerting the subject or not being able to watch at all.

When using an automobile for an observation post, utilizing more than one vantage point is often desirable if more than one point is available. By using multiple vantage points, the investigator can avoid being at any one location for prolonged periods of time. Moving from one vantage point to the next should be accomplished without leaving the subject's area unobserved, even for only a very brief period of time. Doing so can result in failure to observe useful activity, and it is possible for the subject to leave the area during the surveillant's absence. Changing vantage points without leaving the subject's area uncovered is not always possible. If there is a second investigator, one can stay behind and watch the subject area while the other moves to the new position. The first investigator can then walk to the new location while the second investigator, again in position, watches the subject area.

When working from an automobile, generally the investigator will not be as obvious if he sits in the passenger's seat and appears to be waiting for the driver. Another consideration is to sit in the back seat with the visors down. High back seats also aid concealment, and a dark-colored interior is better than a light one. If the car is at an angle to the subject and the investigator is sitting in the rear seat, he should try to position himself so as not to be a silhouette.

Another useful consideration when it is necessary to work from an automobile is to have a clipboard and some preprinted "Traffic Volume Survey" forms handy. A mechanical counter may or may not be used also. This is called *using a pretext*. In the event that someone should ask what the surveillant is doing, that someone could be told that a traffic volume survey is being conducted. To look official, the investigator can use a preprinted survey form with the name of some nonexistent firm at the top.

When using a pretext, the investigator should *never* use the name of an existing firm, nor should he offer the pretext story if approached by a law enforcement officer. In fact, it is desirable in many instances for the investigator to contact the local law enforcement authorities ahead of time, identify himself, and advise them what is taking place. The police should not, however, be given details of the case such as the name of the client or subject. Appropriately notifying the police ahead of time helps to prevent an alert police officer from inquiring why the investigator is loitering in the area, and it helps in the event that someone in the area becomes suspicious and telephones a complaint to the police.

When an automobile will be used for surveillance, it should be a subtle color and a make that one would expect to see in the particular locale. The vehicle should also be free of distinguishing marks or features. Moving into position must be accomplished in an inconspicuous manner, a manner that would be expected of someone who belonged in the area.

Vans and Campers as Observation Posts

When a suitable observation post is not available and when working from an automobile would attract too much attention, a van or camper can prove highly effective. This is especially true when the investigator must work with photographic equipment.

Vans and campers have proven ideal for stationary surveillance work for two reasons. First, the very nature of these vehicles is such that the surveillant can set up inside, with or without optical equipment, and make observations and/or photographs without alerting people outside the vehicle. Second, these vehicles are now so common that they are seen almost everywhere, which means that their use for surveillance purposes is not normally restricted to certain areas.

Opinions differ among investigators as to the best way to equip trucks so that observations can be made from within them. Some prefer to use one-way glass. One-way glass is also referred to as *two-way glass, one-way mirror, x-ray mirror,* or *transparent mirror.* All terms, however, refer to the same product, which is simply clear glass upon whose surface a coating of special metallic silver has been applied. The coating is applied to one side of the glass only and is applied thinly enough to see through but greatly reduce the amount of light that the glass will transmit. The glass, therefore, is only partially transparent.

Perhaps the most frequent argument against the use of one-way glass is that its mirror effect can alert a wary subject to the purpose of the vehicle. One firm attempted to alleviate this problem by painting the name of a fictitious TV repair service on the side of the truck, with a picture of a television set whose screen had been fitted with one-way glass.

Investigators who prefer to avoid the use of one-way glass have devised a number of other methods that have proven to be effective. Some have painted a ficticious business name on the vehicle's windows (painting first a dark background), leaving small holes, perhaps the center of a letter, through which observations and/or photographs can be made. Also effective is using curtains to darken the interior, leaving a small opening through which observations or photographs can be made. In yet other instances, investigators have fashioned *blinds* out of such objects as boxes, paint cans, etc. The blind is placed against the window through which the investigator desires to observe, remaining windows being covered with additional blinds or curtains. The blinds must, naturally, contain camouflaged peep holes. The surveillant may also sit in an enclosed van and look or photograph through the windshield. Finally, if he has mechanical ability, the investigator can make a periscope and camouflage its upper end in an air vent on top of the truck; such devices are also available commercially.

When the investigator is working from a truck or van, he must make every effort to remain perfectly quiet, so that people outside the vehicle do not become aware that the vehicle is occupied. An insulated vehicle helps in this respect. He should also refrain from smoking as that, too, could alert someone.

When the surveillance is to be conducted for any great length of time, provisions should be made for food, drink, and a sanitary facility of some type. For food and drink, a common ice chest will do fine.

The most natural method of moving into the area is for one investigator to hide in the vehicle while a second investigator drives into position, parks, and then walks away. The vehicle will then appear unoccupied. This is much better than the driver remaining in the vehicle after parking it.

Rooms in Nearby Buildings

Often the most desirable vantage point is a room in a building that offers an unobstructed view of the area of interest. Such a room may be a rented apartment or office space, or in more exceptional cases it may be possible for the investigator to persuade a business owner to allow him to use the premises during nonbusiness hours. If a room or office is to be rented for surveillance purposes, it is rarely necessary to inform the proprietor of the operation. However, if an attempt is made to secure permission from a business owner to use the premises for surveillance purposes, it will generally be necessary to explain the purpose, although no details regarding the case should be given. Before approaching anyone on such a matter, the investigator should carefully appraise their degree of trustworthiness, and anyone contacted must be made to understand the need for maintaining complete secrecy about the operation. Generally, although law enforcement investigators frequently use business places for stationary surveillance during nonbusiness hours, private investigators rarely do, but the possibility should not be overlooked when other opportunities do not present themselves.

When working from within a room, every effort should be made to avoid being observed from outside. There are several ways in which this can be accomplished. In all instances it is desirable to darken the room as much as possible; in some instances darkening the room is all that may be necessary. If simply darkening the room is not in itself sufficient, drawing the drapery partway may accomplish the task. The investigator can also make photographs and observations through venetian blinds without being unnecessarily visible from the outside. If there are no draperies but rather curtains or shades, every effort should be made to photograph or observe through a clearance of a couple of inches above or below. The investigator should *never* make observations by pulling a curtain or shade to the side, however, as the movement and unnatural position will attract attention. Finally, when working from a darkened room, it is advisable to stand several feet away from the window.

The usefulness of blinds for surveillance trucks was already discussed; they can also be used when working from a room. A large plant in the window, whether on a stand or hanging, will have a tendency to break up the surveillant's outline. In some instances he may find it desirable to position a mirror so as to make outside observations without being visible. Also, the investigator must remember that nothing will betray his presence more quickly than movement. Finally, as is the case with any vantage point, a discreet means of coming and going must be established, so that attention is not drawn to the operation.

The desirability of any particular technique will always depend upon the particulars of each case, and it is the investigator's task to decide when each is most appropriate. The inexperienced will find it advantageous to try the various techniques at home to get a feel for them before actually attempting to use them on the job.

Rooftops as Observation Posts

If not so high that the investigator is looking down onto the subject at an extreme angle, rooftops can be effectively used as vantage points.

As in the case when working from an automobile, a position on the next block is desirable when working from a rooftop because there will be much less chance of being noticed by the subject. It is also important for the investigator to avoid being silhouetted against the sky, by keeping something such as a chimney or air conditioner behind himself. The importance of this point cannot be overemphasized.

When the investigator is working from rooftops, weather conditions will be an important factor. Inclement weather not only leads to discomfort but can in many instances limit the use of certain pieces of optical equipment that would be damaged by the moisture.

When considering rooftops, it is important for the investigator to consider the means by which he will get to and leave the roof. In many instances access to a roof is locked; if it is not locked, there is always the likelihood of someone such as a custodian or maintainance person discovering the activity. In this instance a pretext may be in order. Additionally, travel to and from the roof must be accomplished in a discreet manner.

Outdoor Observation Posts

Several possibilities for observation posts for stationary surveillance have so far been discussed — automobiles, vans and campers, rooms in nearby buildings, and rooftops. When none of those methods are appropriate for some reason, the investigator must consider using an outdoor observation post. When using an outdoor observation post, a *pretext* will often be in order. The type of pretext most likely to be successful will depend upon the nature of the area in which it will be used, the duration of time that the surveillance must be conducted, and the investigator's ability to carry out the pretext.

The investigator's ability to carry out the pretext successfully does not depend on his ability as an investigator so much as his knowledge of the pretext being used. He should utilize a pretext that is simple and that he has enough knowledge of to successfully act the part.

For short-term surveillance, the investigator might consider raising the hood of his car and tinkering with the engine to simulate mechanical problems, thus becoming a stalled motorist in the eyes of others in the area. He may also use the pretext of conducting a traffic volume survey, mentioned earlier. Another pretext role that may be considered is that of a surveyor. Using this pretext would naturally require possession of at least a basic understanding of surveying.

When utilizing pretext it is desirable that it be subtle, so that the investigator can remain as unnoticed as possible. A pretext should never call attention to the investigator; rather, it should offer a logical reason for lingering in the area.

FOOT SURVEILLANCE

General Techniques and Methods

Foot surveillance is following a person while walking from one location to another. A foot surveillance can be very basic, requiring a lone investigator to follow a subject while trying to remain undetected, or it can be a complex operation utilizing a well-coordinated team of two or three investigators. When they are working as a team, each of the investigators has a specific position in relation to that of the subject and other members of the team. A well-coordinated surveillance team can be highly effective, but, if a team is not well coordinated, the results will generally be poor. Preplanning and practice are necessary.

Foot surveillance generally begins with stationary surveillance while the investigator waits for the subject to appear. Foot surveillance can also require stationary techniques during intermittent stops and at the subject's final destination.

The investigator conducting foot surveillance faces two principal risks: losing the subject and being discovered. However, the more familiar the investigator is with the subject and the locale within which the surveillance is being conducted, the less chance there will be of either of these two situations occurring. Additionally, the more information the investigator has regarding the subject, the better will be the chances of reestablishing contact in the event that the subject is lost.

The identification of the subject is the most important element of any surveillance operation in which an individual is to be followed. Doing everything correctly from start to finish will avail nothing if the wrong person is followed. That is why it is so important that *all* identifying data pertaining to the subject be obtained and verified before the surveillance is actually attempted. The client will often be in possession of the necessary information. When this is not the case, however, the investigator must develop it. The time spent developing such information is generally time well spent.

The most reliable method by which to ensure that the right person is followed is to have someone point the subject out. When this is done, the person designating the subject should not be seen by the subject. This is especially important if the designator is known to the subject. Once the designation has been made, the designator should leave the area at the first opportunity. When it is not possible to have someone designate the subject, a recent photograph along with a thorough physical description is useful.

Before attempting foot surveillance, the investigator should obtain an ample supply of expense money, including plenty of small change, so that he can readily go where the subject goes.

Because when conducting foot surveillance the investigator is generally viewing the subject from behind, he should note carefully the subject's appearance from that angle, as well as any peculiarities regarding the walk or posture. He must learn to follow the person, not the clothing. A subject can utilize disguise techniques such as a reversible jacket and/or cap, or a complete change of clothing may at some point be made. A change of clothing will not alter the subject's height, weight, posture, or way of walking, however, and the surveillant should be alert to these things.

When the subject begins moving from the area the surveillant should not change position until certain that the subject is in fact leaving. It is important to guard against premature movement because a subject will, at times, in an effort to detect a surveillant, reverse direction while carefully studying the reaction of others in the area. Should the investigator fall victim to such a tactic, he should, when the subject stops or reverses direction, continue on in a natural manner. If it is possible to later reposition himself discreetly so as to resume the surveillance, it should be done. In the event that this cannot be done in a discreet manner, the surveillance should be discontinued until another time.

When beginning the surveillance, the investigator should move to the vantage point in a manner that will appear natural to anyone who may be in the area. Sudden or unnatural movement on anyone's part will almost always attract attention. If a pretext is used to justify being in the area, it should be of such a nature that hurried packing of equipment is not necessary, as that will serve to attract unwanted attention.

When conducting the surveillance, the most appropriate distance to be maintained between the surveillant and the subject will be determined largely by the conditions as they exist at the time. The investigator must remain close enough to the subject to avoid losing contact and effectively observe actions but remain far enough away to avoid detection. On a street relatively free of pedestrian traffic, it may be necessary for him to remain a distance of half a city block, or more, away from the subject. On a very crowded street, however, it may be necessary to remain as close as ten feet or less.

When the subject turns a corner, every effort should be made to reach the corner quickly without attracting attention. This is important because if too much time is lost, the subject may enter a building before the surveillant can get to the corner. If, when he reaches the corner, he does not see the subject the investigator should attempt to determine what door may have been entered based upon the subject's speed, the location of the doors, and the time interval between the subject's reaching the corner and his own arrival at the same corner. In the event that the surveillant turns the corner only to discover that the subject has stopped and the two are face to face, he should show no sign of surprise or recognition and make no eye contact but rather should continue on his way as if nothing were wrong. He should then attempt to discreetly reestablish a position behind the subject when the opportunity presents itself.

In the event that the subject enters a building, the nature of both the building and the case will generally determine whether following the subject inside is appropriate. Should the subject enter a busy department store, for example, it would most likely be appropriate to follow. However, should the subject enter a barber shop or some small store where there are very few customers at any given time, it may be desirable to wait outside and resume the surveillance when the subject reappears. When watching a building from a position at a corner, it is possible to observe *two* sides of the building at one time.

A subject who enters a hotel lobby but is nowhere in sight once inside may have gone directly to the men's or women's room, and a check should be made if possible. Should the subject go to the desk to inquire about a room, the investigator should attempt to get in line and overhear what is said.

Should the subject enter a bar or nightclub, it is important that the surveillant also enter before anyone can be seated. If the subject is seated it may be difficult to ascertain exactly where he is, because a bar's interior lighting is generally subdued, the subject may be sitting with a group of people, the establishment may be reasonably crowded, and, depending upon the time of year, coats and head coverings may be removed thus altering general appearances. Exactly where the surveillant should position himself in relation to the subject must be decided upon at the time. The most suitable position is naturally one that affords a view of the subject without being conspicuous. A position toward the rear of the establishment tends to afford a view of the entire area, and the investigator can observe people as they enter and leave.

When entering a bar, the investigator should determine where to sit without unusual delay so as to avoid drawing attention. In some instances, if there is more than one investigator assigned to the case, it will be desirable for the first investigator to enter the bar, appraise the situation, and then leave, allowing the second investigator to enter and, benefiting from what the first investigator has learned, go without hesitation to the desired position.

If at some point the subject boards a bus, the surveillant should also board, a short distance behind, and attempt to select a seat a short distance to the subject's rear. This will not be possible, however, if the subject selects a back seat. Should the subject sit in a seat that is positioned lengthwise, the surveillant should attempt to sit on the same side of the vehicle a few seats away.

Simple disguise techniques are useful when following a subject. The investigator can alter his general appearance by such simple means as a reversible jacket, glasses with both clear and dark lenses, and a hat. To be avoided, however, are theatrical types of disguises.

Finally, the surveillant should have some idea as to what he will use for an excuse or explanation regarding his activities if at some point the subject should become suspicious and a confrontation should result. In some instances an act of indignation will be appropriate, while in others a pretext, possibly supported with fictitious credentials, may be appropriate.

Multiple-Person Surveillance Teams

The effectiveness of a foot surveillance operation can be greatly increased by using more than one investigator. The usual positioning of the investigators in relation to each other and to the subject, as depicted in Figure 4-2, is to have one investigator (1) follow the subject (S), with a second investigator (2) following Investigator 1. A third investigator (3) is across the street paralleling the subject. When only two investigators are available, position 2 is generally eliminated.

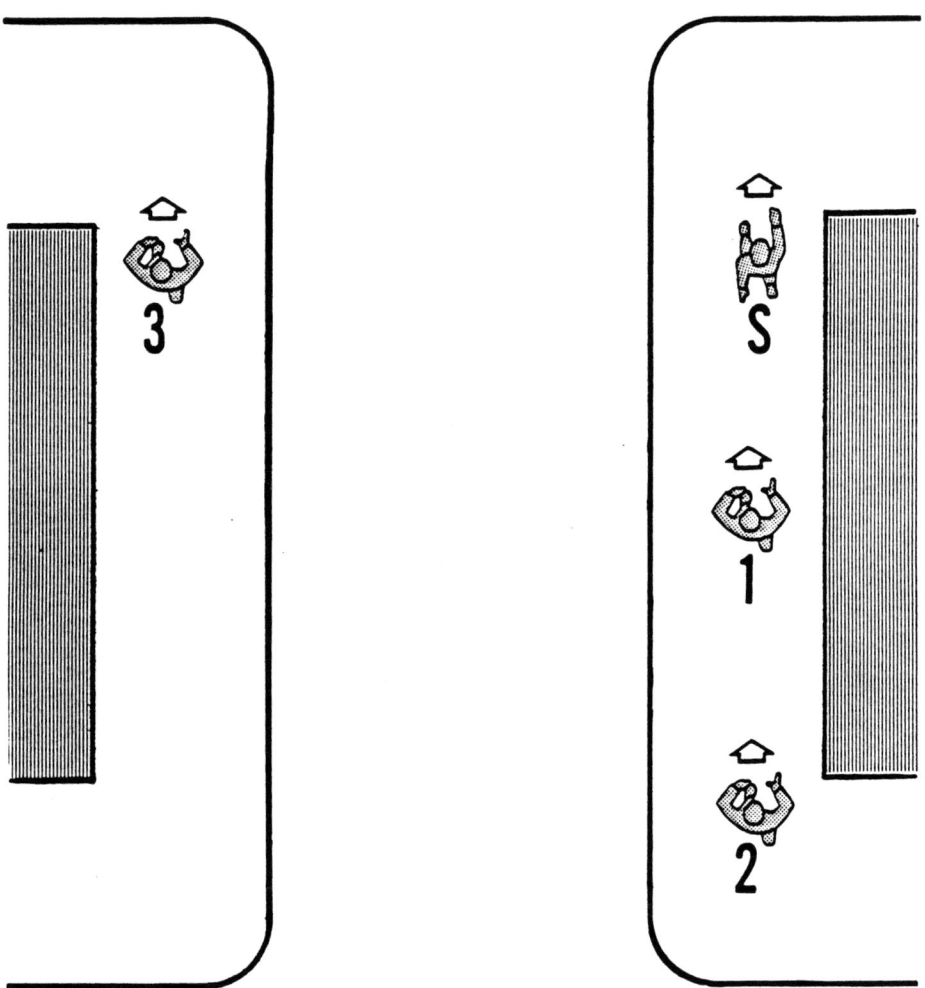

Figure 4-2. A typical multiple-person foot surveillance technique involves having one investigator (1) follow the subject (S), with a second investigator (2) following Investigator 1. A third investigator (3) walks abreast of the subject. If only two investigators are assigned to the case, position 2 is generally eliminated.

Utilizing more than one investigator means that the investigators can trade positions frequently to avoid having one person behind the subject for prolonged periods of time. This can be accomplished if the investigator in position 2 increases speed while Investigator 1 steps into a doorway or slows down, whichever seems appropriate under the circumstances. Positions may also be rotated smoothly each time the subject turns a corner. Ideas for how this can be accomplished are illustrated in Figures 4-3, 4-4, 4-5, and 4-6.

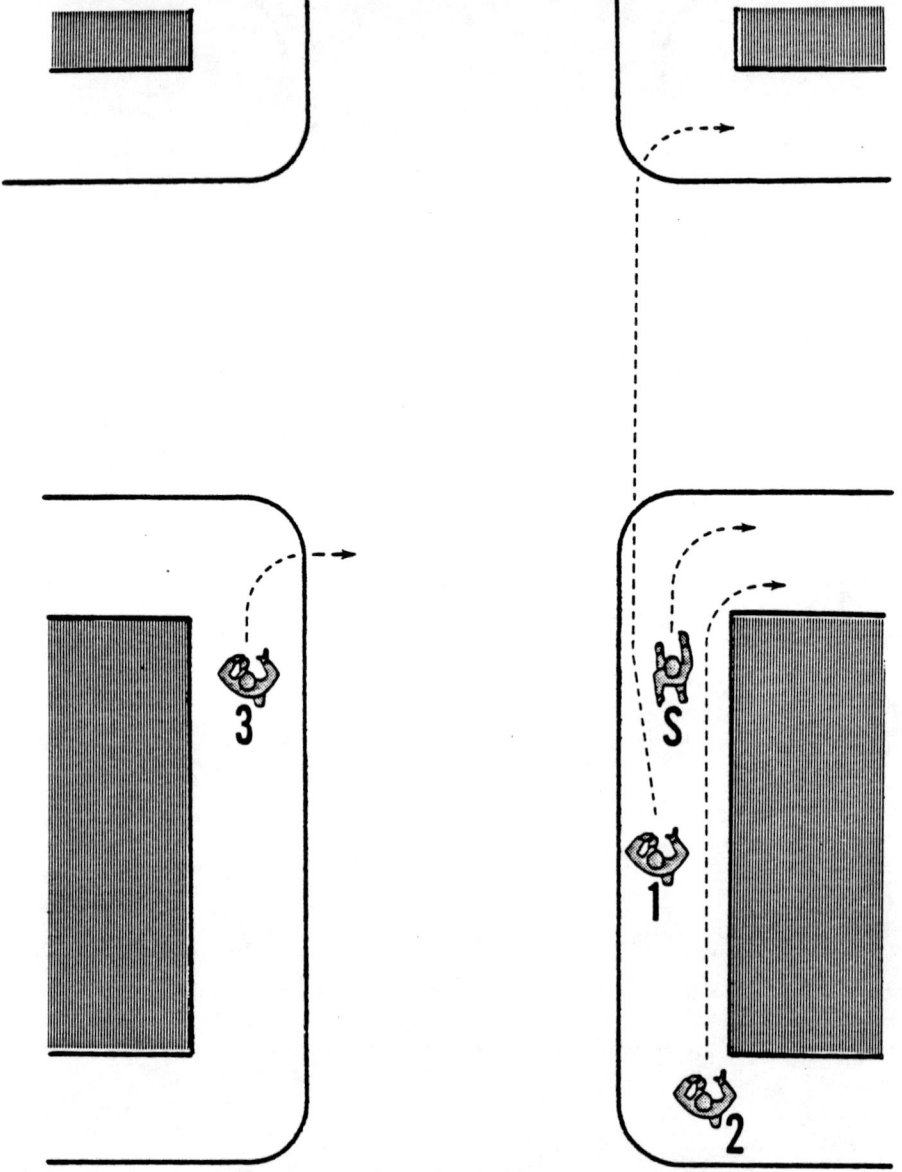

Figure 4-3. Subject turns right before crossing the intersection. Investigator 1 crosses the intersection, thus assuming the 3 position. Investigator 2 turns the corner and assumes the 1 position. Investigator 3 assumes the 2 position.

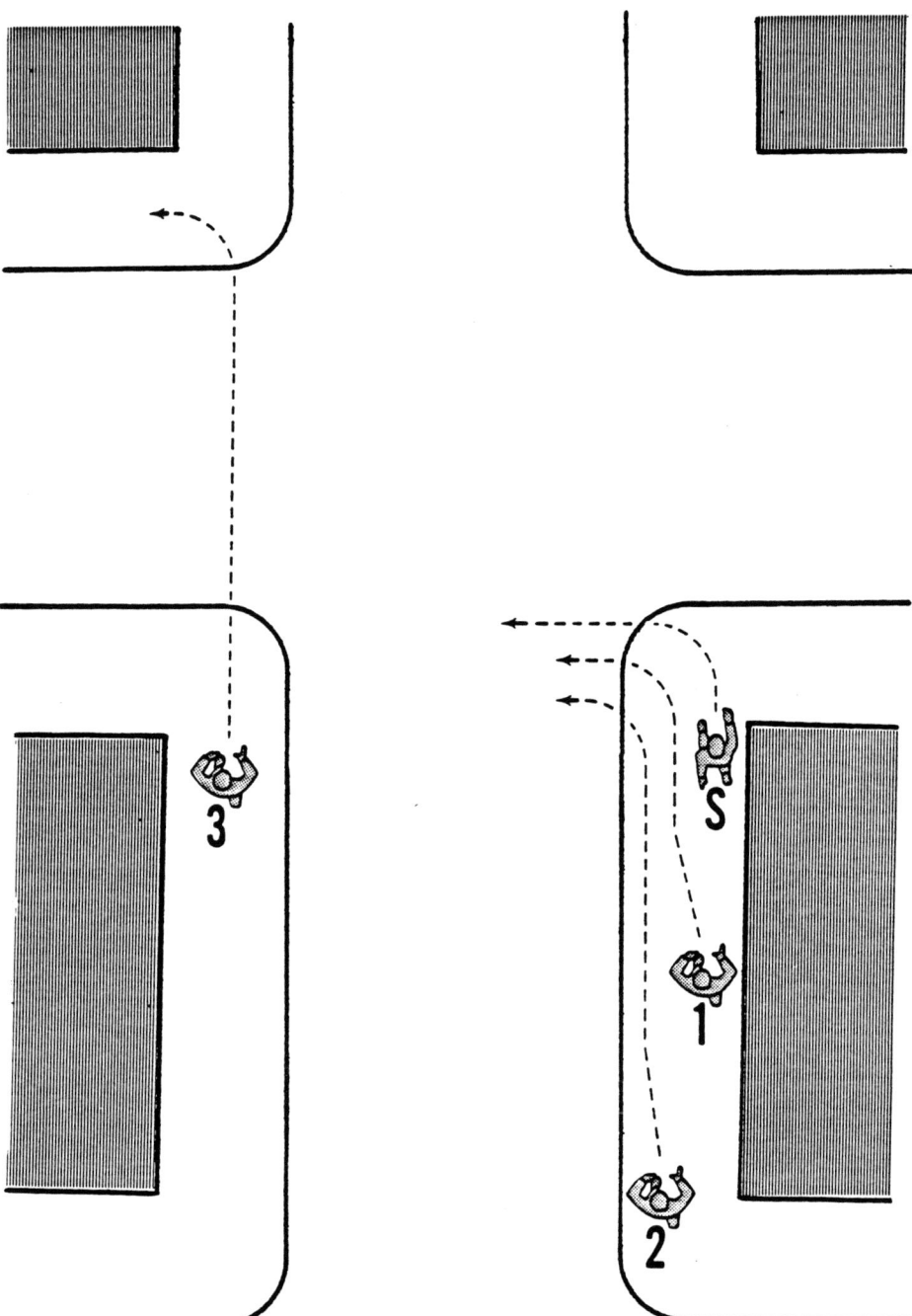

Figure 4-4. Subject turns left before crossing the intersection. Investigator 1 follows the subject, while Investigator 2 follows 1. Investigator 3 crosses and turns left. All have maintained their original position, except that investigator 3 is now on the opposite side of the subject.

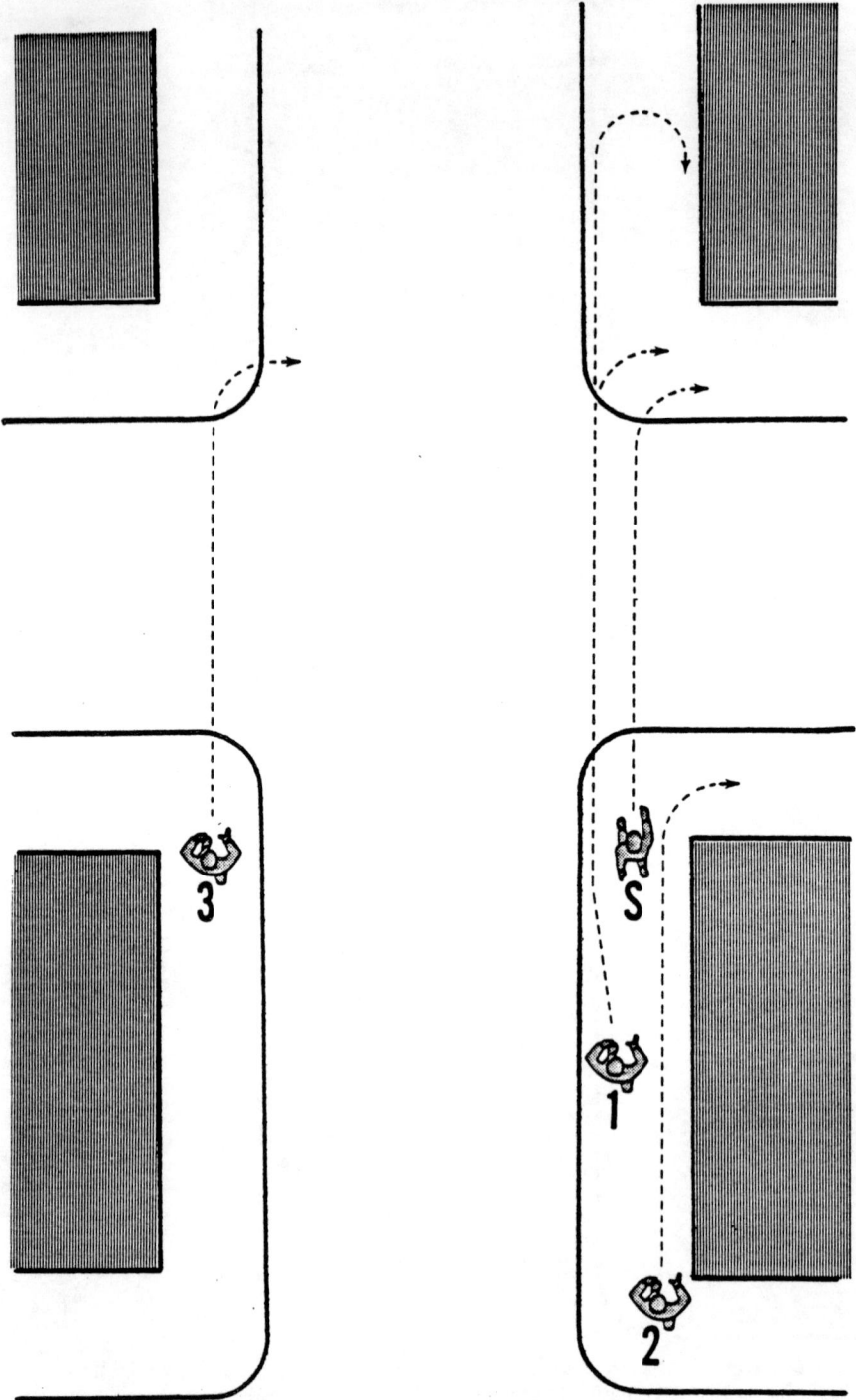

Figure 4-5. Subject crosses the intersection and turns right. Investigator 1 crosses and either turns right, thus maintaining the 1 position, or goes straight only to double back and assume the 2 position after Investigator 3 has taken the lead position. Investigator 2 turns before crossing, thus assuming the 3 position.

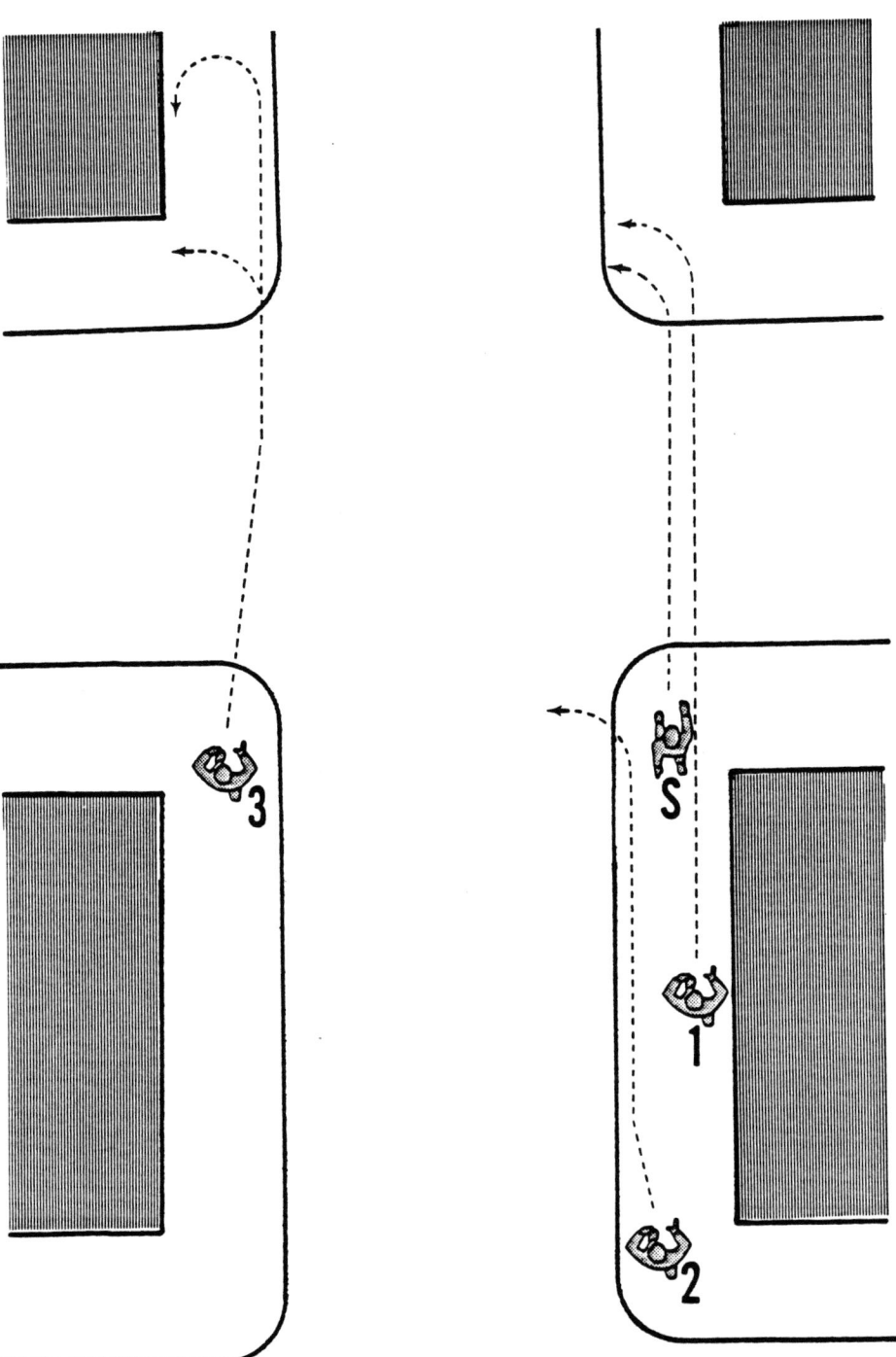

Figure 4-6. Subject crosses the interesection and turns left. Investigator 1 follows. Investigator 2 turns before crossing, thus assuming the 3 position. Investigator 3 crosses the intersection and either turns left, thus assuming the 1 position, or goes straight only to double back to assume the 2 position.

Should the subject turn a corner and immediately enter a building, the investigator in the parallel position (3) will be able to observe the fact and can signal the other members of the team accordingly.

A subject who fears being surveilled will often engage in a variety of actions that are designed to detect and/or elude the follower. The following are some typical actions in which a subject may engage and some appropriate responses on the part of the investigator. These are presented as ideas only, as each individual will act differently, and the appropriate response on the part of the investigator will naturally depend upon the specific circumstances.

Subject's Action	*Surveillant's Response*
1. Stops after turning corner to study reaction of other people as they reach corner.	1. Proceeds on as if nothing is wrong
2. Boards a public conveyance such as a bus and then quickly jumps off as it is about to depart	2. Rides the bus to the next stop, gets off, and then boards the next bus (Subject may be on it.)
3. Enters a building only to leave by another exit	3. Either follows the subject inside or positions himself at a corner to observe exits on two sides of the building
4. Has a partner follow him in an effort to detect surveillance (called a *convoy*)	4. Follows the convoy, as it will go where the subject goes (should always be alert for a convoy)
5. Drops a scrap of paper to see if anyone attempts to pick it up	5. Attempts to casually kick the paper to the side for later retrieval (If there is a second investigator, retrival will be easier)
6. Walks at irregular pace	6. Attempts to settle on an average speed
7. Takes a suicidal chance crossing a busy street	7. Does not take such chances
8. Reverses direction of travel and studies the people met	8. Continues past the subject and considers repositioning himself or discontinuing the surveillance (if using multiple-person technique, should rotate the position of the members)
9. Goes through a large open area such as a parking lot or park, or uses such a location for a meeting	9. Watches from a distance and/or attempts to go around the area

10. Approaches the investigator and accuses him of following

10. Acts indignant and denies the charge or offers a preplanned cover story that may be supported with fictitious props and/or credentials

AUTOMOBILE SURVEILLANCE

Introduction

When attempting to follow a subject who utilizes some type of vehicle for transportation, the investigator, naturally, must utilize a vehicle as well. There are many techniques for this type of surveillance, variations of which may be used depending upon the circumstances involved.

Many factors will determine the most appropriate technique, but the investigator must have a clear understanding of the merits of each technique to effectively determine which one or variation thereof is most appropriate in any given situation.

Any automobile surveillance should begin with a preliminary survey of the area in which the surveillance is expected to begin. In many instances it will be desirable to have the survey made by someone other than the investigator, so that someone residing in the area does not notice and later recognize the investigator. The preliminary survey will enable the investigator to make sound decisions as to the type of vehicle appropriate for the area and the most suitable mode of dress; it will enable him to give some thought as to where he will position himself while waiting for the subject to appear; and it will help him to anticipate what, if any, equipment may be needed, such as binoculars, telescopes, and radios.

When considering what type of vehicle will be most appropriate, the investigator will generally find that a vehicle of a common make, such as Ford or Chevrolet, reasonably new, with no distinguishing features, and of a subtle color is quite appropriate. Bright colors such as red and yellow stand out and should be avoided. As for dress, sports clothing will generally be the most versatile. It is not a bad idea for the surveillant to wear sports clothing and have a sport coat and tie in the car, so that it will be available should he find it necessary to follow the subject into some establishment where a jacket and tie are appropriate.

When the investigator is choosing a point from which to watch for the subject, it is important that he anticipate which route may be used to leave the area and what the most suitable course of action will be. This is very important, because in many cases a subject is lost within the first few blocks because of poor planning and positioning on the investigator's part.

In some instances, no position will be available that offers both a view of the subject's vehicle and the opportunity to begin the surveillance easily when that vehicle moves. When this is the case, it will generally be necessary to have one investigator with a radio observe the subject and/or the vehicle, while another investigator or investigators will be positioned at location(s) that will enable him or them to begin the surveillance when advised by the first investigator of the subject's movement.

Unfortunately, it is often necessary to conduct a vehicle surveillance alone because a client or employer will not agree to the added expense of assigning two vehicles and investigators to a case. However, when two vehicles can be used, the effectiveness of the operation and the chances for successful results are increased appreciably. This is because the vehicles can frequently trade positions in relation to the subject, thus avoiding having any one vehicle behind the subject for prolonged periods of time. More than one vehicle also helps to prevent a broken surveillance in the event that one of the surveillance vehicles develops mechanical problems.

When more than one vehicle has been assigned to the operation, one vehicle will actually follow the subject while the other vehicle(s) will assume position(s) either to the rear of the lead vehicle, abreast of the subject on parallel streets, or perhaps in front of the subject, depending upon factors such as the layout of the streets. The use of more than one vehicle for surveillance will be discussed in greater detail later in this chapter.

It is important that the investigator doing the driving on any automobile surveillance be an experienced and highly capable driver who can react quickly yet safely to the ever-changing traffic conditions. This is especially important when traffic is heavy. It is also important that the driver be willing to drive *very* aggressively at times to avoid losing the subject. Finally, regardless of how experienced the driver may be, it is essential that he be familiar with the handling characteristics of the vehicle being driven.

The most basic vehicle surveillance technique involves one vehicle driven by one investigator attempting to follow a subject. In this endeavor there are a number of proven techniques and methods that can be employed.

The most appropriate distance to be maintained between the investigator's vehicle and the subject's will depend largely upon the topographical conditions of the area and upon existing traffic conditions. The distance can vary from little more than one car length during heavy intercity work traffic to distances of half a city block or more on streets that are almost void of traffic. On freeways, the distance will be greater, and in the country, an experienced investigator can follow a vehicle successfully from as much as a mile away at times.

If there is more than one lane for traffic traveling in each direction, a lane next to that being used by the subject is desirable, so long as traffic conditions are not so heavy as to prohibit it. Also desirable is allowing an unrelated vehicle (never more than one) to come between the investigator and the subject. However, in heavy traffic, that, too, can result in losing the subject.

When following a subject in an urban environment, the investigator must be alert to traffic control signals and anticipate their pending status. When approaching a green signal light, for example, the distance between the subject and the investigator should be reduced to prevent having the subject go through the intersection on a green or yellow light while the investigator is faced with a red light.

In the event that the surveillant does get caught at a red traffic light, he has the option of either waiting for it to turn green, which could result in losing the subject, bypassing the light as shown in Figure 4-7, or simply disobeying the light. If the decision is made to disobey the light, this must be done giving full regard to the right-of-way and safety of other motorists. The fact that the investigator is conducting a surveillance does not make disobeying a traffic light legal, nor will it serve as a defense against a civil or criminal suit should his actions result in an accident.

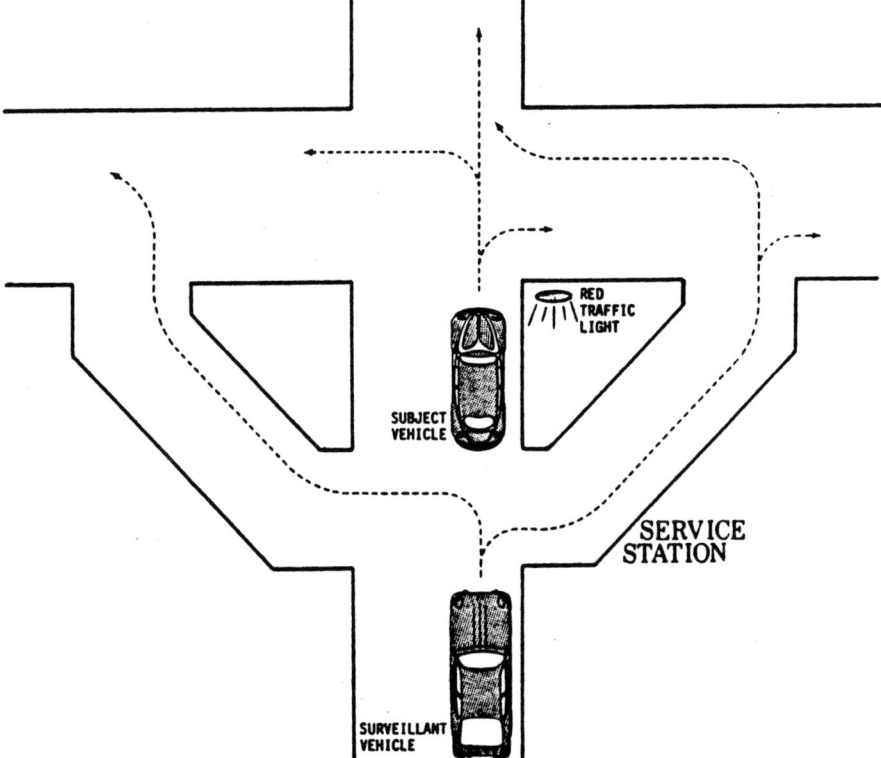

Figure 4-7. When a traffic light turns red after a subject passes through the intersection or executes a turn but before the investigator arrives at the light, he may either stop for the light, disobey it, or bypass it by going through the service station or parking lot as depicted.

If the investigator does disobey a traffic light, it is important that he do so without the subject's being aware of it. That will not always be possible, however. A common method used either to detect or to elude a surveillant is to time the arrival at a controlled intersection so that all traffic to the rear must stop for a red light. The subject, once clearing the intersection, simply observes traffic to the rear to see who disobeys the red light. *It must also be emphasized that this chapter is in no way suggesting that the reader violate traffic laws while conducting a surveillance.*

When the subject turns into a parking lot, it is better to proceed on and use the next entrance rather than follow directly using the same entrance. Similarly, in the event that the subject parks on the street, there is less chance of being noticed by the subject and arousing unwanted suspicion by proceeding on and parking a short distance ahead.

When following a vehicle on a multilaned freeway, the investigator must guard against becoming blocked by traffic so as to prevent being able to exit behind the subject when an exit ramp is taken. The best way to guard against this is to avoid traveling more than one lane from the exit lane unless traffic is very light.

When heavy traffic conditions require that the investigator remain very close to the subject's vehicle, every effort should be made to stay within the blind spots. When driving in another motorist's blind spot, he must remain very alert and ready to take evasive action in the event that the other driver changes lanes unaware that there is a vehicle in the path. Many accidents have resulted from this very occurrence.

A number of simple techniques can alter the general appearance of a person (as already discussed) *or a vehicle* to decrease the possibility of the subject's becoming aware that the same person and/or vehicle is consistently in his vicinity. The props necessary to effect a change of appearance are not costly or difficult to employ, and the investigator should have them available whenever an automobile surveillance is conducted.

The general appearance of a vehicle can be altered somewhat by raising and lowering visors, placing or removing objects from the dash, and hanging and removing items from the rearview mirror. If two or more investigators are in one vehicle, they can occasionally alter their seating arrangement, or one or more investigators can lie down, thus giving the appearance of varying numbers of occupants. At night, proper use of various cutout switches for lights is effective. Such switches can make it appear that a car with two headlamps is following the subject for a while and then later a vehicle with a burned-out headlamp is behind the subject. At various times the parking lights can also be added or eliminated.

When something is done to alter the general appearance of a person or vehicle, care must be exercised to accomplish the change out of view of the subject, or the purpose of the disguise will be defeated.

Earlier it was stated that the effectiveness of a vehicle surveillance can be improved by utilizing two or more vehicles. When assigning more than one vehicle to a surveillance cannot be accomplished, the next best thing is assigning two investigators to one vehicle. This will allow the driver to concentrate fully on the important task of driving while the second investigator concentrates on the subject and directs the driver. The second investigator can also record notes and follow the subject on foot if necessary when a destination is reached. When this is done, the driver will usually remain to watch the subject's vehicle.

In instances where a subject turns a corner and proceeds on while the investigators are tied up in traffic and thus not in a position to see where the subject goes, the second investigator can go to the corner on foot to observe the subject's movements until the surveillance vehicle can get to the corner and resume the surveillance (*see* Figure 4-8).

When conducting a motor vehicle surveillance, the investigator should be alert for indications that the subject has become aware of being followed. The new and inexperienced investigator is almost always prone to think that he has been detected when in fact he has not; experience helps him overcome that feeling and enables him to determine better when he has been detected.

Exactly what the surveillant should do when he has been detected by a subject will depend upon the circumstances and the policy of the firm by which he is employed. In almost all cases, however, he should discontinue the surveillance.

When watching for signs of having been detected, the investigator should not be deceived or misled when a subject executes routine maneuvers to lose anyone who *may* be following. Many subjects will routinely engage in such activity as a precautionary measure.

Parallel Surveillance

When the amount of traffic is very light and attempting to follow a vehicle from behind would likely result in detection, the investigator should consider the feasibility of paralleling the subject. Not all locales will favor such a technique, however, and for it to be effective, the investigator must be extremely familiar with the layout of the area.

When paralleling a subject, the investigator travels in the same direction as the subject on a parallel street one block away. He will attempt to spot the subject at an intersection and then move rapidly to the next intersection and again watch for the subject's arrival. This process is continued until the subject either reaches an intersection and turns or fails to show up at an intersection.

When the subject reaches an intersection and turns toward the investigator, he may proceed through the intersection and turn on the next block to assume, once again, a parallel position. If the subject turns in the opposite direction after reaching an intersection, the surveillant will generally find it necessary to turn the same direction. Generally, he may reassume a parallel position when the subject turns again.

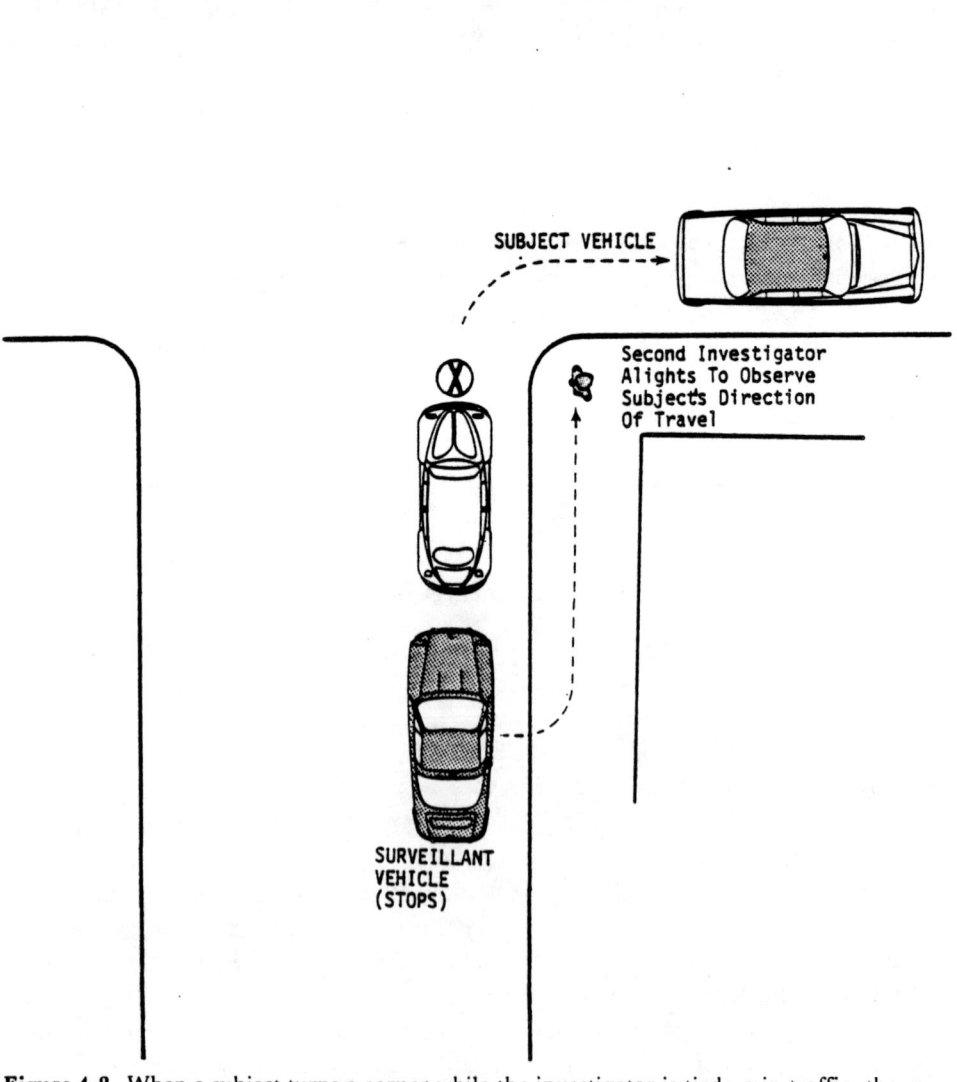

Figure 4-8. When a subject turns a corner while the investigator is tied up in traffic, the second investigator can alight and go on foot to the corner to observe the subject's movements.

When the subject being paralled fails to show up at an intersection, it means that he may have made a turn into an alley or a driveway, or the vehicle may have been parked along the street. The surveillant will then turn towards that intersection in an effort to determine the subject's location.

Progressive Surveillance

A progressive surveillance technique is employed when a subject is unusually wary or when the case is of such extreme importance that all measures must be taken to ensure that the subject does not become aware of being the object of a surveillance.

This method of surveillance is useful and will provide successful results in instances where a subject consistently travels the *same route* to the *same destination*. Additionally, this method of surveillance can be employed equally well whether the operation is being conducted on foot or with a vehicle.

This type of surveillance is conducted, just as its name implies, in a progressive manner. For example:

First Day: A subject is observed leaving home, and the direction of travel is noted; the investigator at this point may or may not follow the subject for a short distance. For the purpose of this example, the subject proceeds on foot to a nearby bus stop and boards a certain bus.

Second Day: An investigator will have gotten on the bus at an earlier stop and will remain on the bus to observe where the subject gets off. Ideally, when the subject gets off, the investigator remains seated and gets off at some subsequent stop.

Third Day: An investigator can be waiting to observe the subject's course of travel *after* getting off the bus and may or may not follow the subject for a short distance.

This process is continued until the desired information has been obtained. The ideal aspect of this method of surveillance is that no one individual is ever with the subject for a prolonged period of time, and no one really appears to be following. When the subject boards the bus and gets off, for example, no one in an investigative capacity gets on or off, and the investigator waiting to follow when the subject does get off the bus is not behind the subject long enough to be detected.

Following a Bicyclist

Following a subject who rides a bicycle is a very difficult task. The difficulty of following a bicyclist results from the fact that the cyclist generally travels too fast to be followed on foot yet too slow to be followed with a vehicle. Additionally, the bicyclist can readily take shortcuts between buildings, can travel against traffic on a one-way street more readily than can a motorist, and can generally violate traffic laws without consequence much more readily than can the driver of a vehicle.

In spite of the many difficulties inherent in following a bicyclist, however, there are a number of techniques that the investigator may consider. As with any surveillance techniques, the appropriateness of any of these will depend upon the specific circumstances involved.

In Figure 4-9 are depicted a subject riding a bicycle and a number of investigators utilizing various surveillance techniques. Naturally, no single surveillance operation would require this many investigators utilizing all these techniques; this illustration presents all the techniques for which an explanation is presented. These explanations will help the investigator to be better prepared to decide what technique will be most appropriate when it is necessary to follow a bicyclist.

At the top of the illustration is depicted a vehicle frequently dropping off an investigator ahead of the subject. The vehicle stops only long enough to make the drop and then drives away, in most instances circling the block. This process is simply repeated as often as necessary. When the investigator is dropped off, it is often desirable to make the drop around a corner out of view of the subject. It is also desirable to employ various disguises such as glasses, hats, wigs, and a reversible jacket or change of shirts.

In the upper right corner of Figure 4-9 is a surveillance vehicle circling the block and spotting the subject at intersections. The drawback of this technique is that the subject is not under constant observation.

On the left side of Figure 4-9 is depicted a surveillance vehicle paralleling the subject by driving slowly on a parallel street one block away. The investigator may be one block to either the right or the left of the subject depending upon the layout of the streets. This technique is the same as paralleling an automobile and suffers from the same limitations.

Below and to the right of the subject is an investigator on a motorcycle. The motorcyclist may parallel the subject, may circle blocks spotting the subject at intersections, or may follow the subject directly by driving at reduced speeds and possibly watching from stationary positions behind a parked vehicle. The motorcyclist would frequently move ahead to assume a position behind another parked vehicle when the distance between the subject and the investigator became too great. When a motorcycle is used in such a situation, a good muffler system should be used to avoid attracting attention.

Finally, another bicycle may be used to follow a bicyclist. The fact that a bicyclist does not have good rear vision helps considerably to avoid detection. The best distance to be maintained will vary depending upon the conditions. Good judgment and experience will generally be the best teachers.

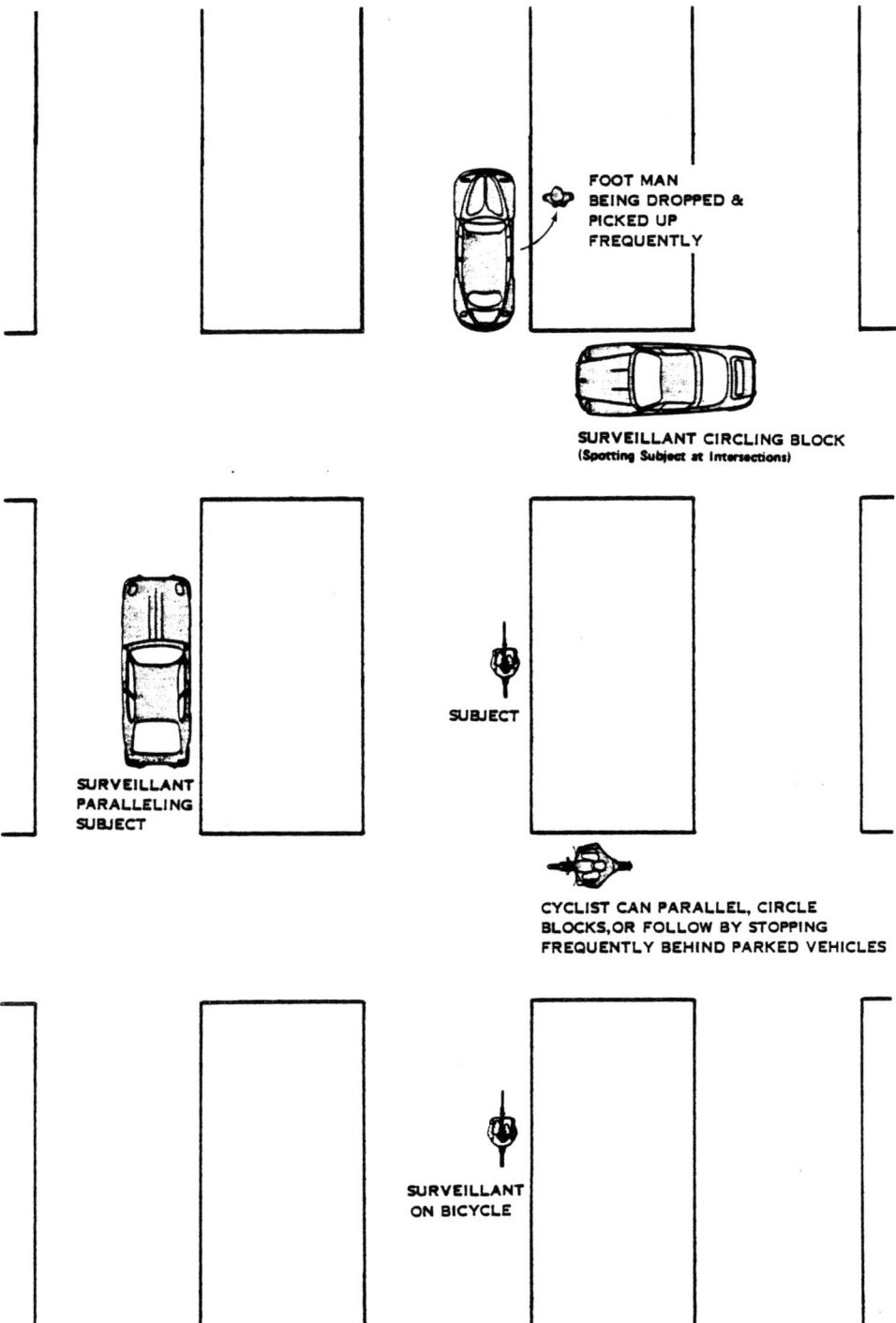

Figure 4-9. Several possibilities for following a bicyclist

Multiple-Vehicle Surveillance Techniques

The most basic multiple-vehicle technique is generally a variation of that depicted in Figure 4-10. In this illustration a subject is followed by a surveillant vehicle and is flanked on both sides by surveillant vehicles on parallel streets one block away. In some instances, there will be a surveillant vehicle preceding the subject, as shown, or that vehicle may be positioned behind the lead vehicle. Naturally, this basic technique would be modified according to the number of investigators and vehicles assigned to the case, the layout of the streets, and the needs of the case.

When positioning the surveillant vehicles so that there are two vehicles following the subject from the rear, it is desirable for those vehicles to frequently rotate their positions in relation to the subject to avoid having either vehicle exposed to the subject's view for prolonged periods of time. This can be accomplished by the second vehicle's increasing speed while the first turns off or slows down. ·

When more than one vehicle is involved in a surveillance, it is very important that provisions be made for effective radio communications between them. If for some reason that is not possible, prearranged signals such as flashing the brake lights may be employed.

When two vehicles are following a subject, the driver of the lead vehicle will utilize the same techniques previously discussed to avoid being detected, including alternating driving habits and utilizing disguise techniques for both himself and the vehicle. Distance generally provides sufficient cover for the second vehicle; however, on straight stretches of road where the amount of traffic is very limited, the driver of the second vehicle should attempt to keep the first vehicle in the line of sight between himself and the subject. That will help to ensure against the subject noticing or studying the vehicle for later recognition.

In the event that the subject makes an unexpected U turn, a tactic to either detect or elude anyone who may be following, it is desirable for the first vehicle to continue straight ahead in a normal manner while relaying the information to the second vehicle. The second vehicle should turn off the road and wait for the subject to pass by and then assume the lead position. The original lead vehicle will, when conditions permit, turn around and assume the number two position (*see* Figure 4-11).

Should the subject turn into an alley, it is generally desirable for the lead vehicle to stop short of the alley, allowing the second investigator to get out (if there is a second investigator in the car) and go on foot to the alley to observe the subject's subsequent movements. Additionally, the second vehicle should be appropriately advised so that a turn can be made a block early, in the same direction as the subject turned (*see* Figure 4-12). In the event that the subject continues through the alley, the second vehicle (that turned a block early) is in

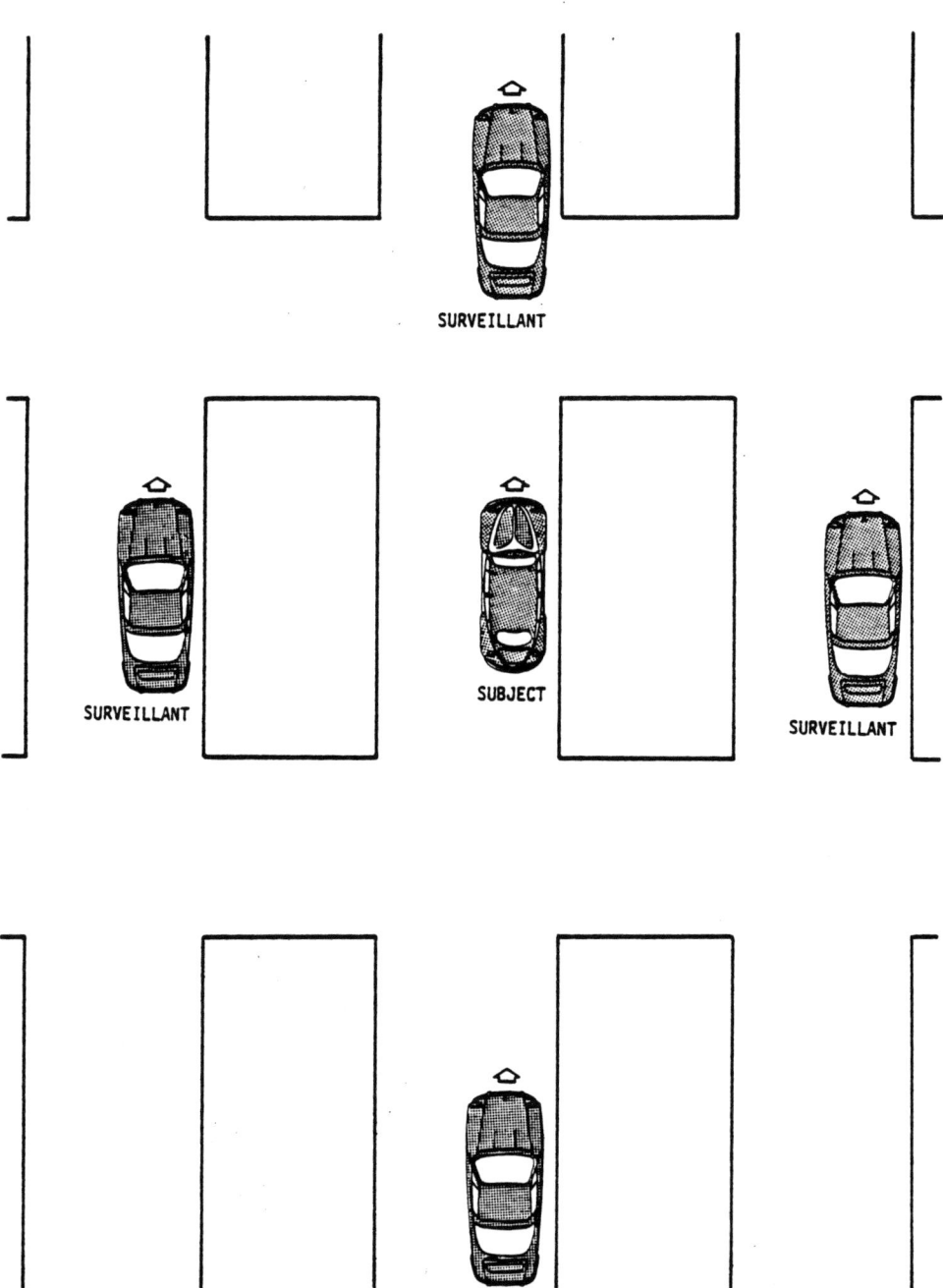

Figure 4-10. A basic multiple-vehicle surveillance technique involves having one or two surveillant vehicles behind the subject and surveillant vehicles flanking the subject on parallel streets. In some instances it may also be desirable to have a surveillant vehicle preceding the subject. This basic technique must, of course, be modified according to the circumstances and topographical conditions involved.

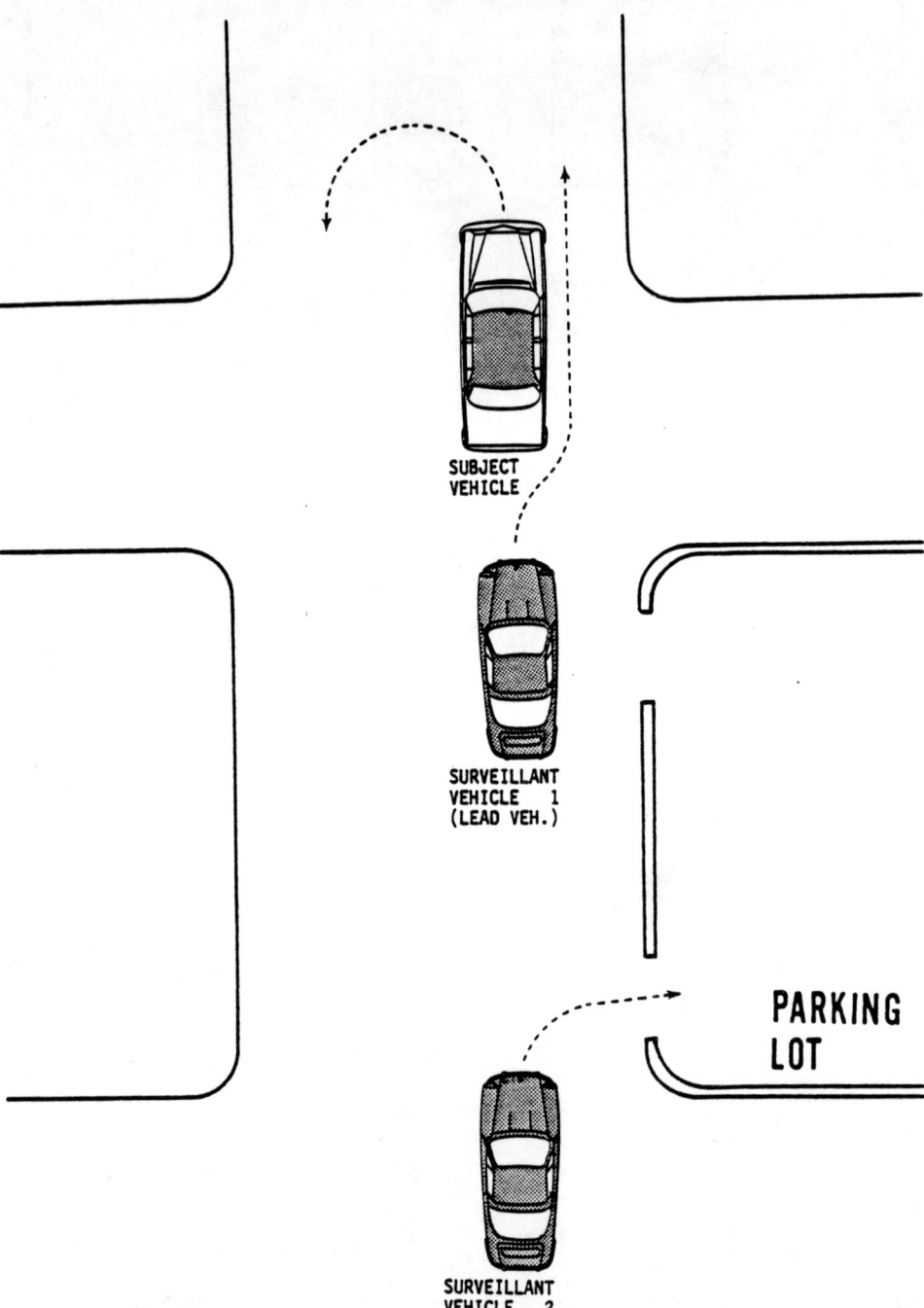

Figure 4-11. Subject makes a U turn. The lead vehicle (1) should continue on and radio to vehicle 2, who will turn off, wait for the subject to pass by, and then assume the lead position. Vehicle 1, which was originally in the lead, will pass from the subject's view, turn around, and assume the 2 position.

position to assume the lead position regardless of which direction the subject may then turn. The original lead vehicle will then assume the second position.

A subject will on occasion stop short or greatly reduce speed just after rounding a curve or passing over the crest of a hill and then observe the reaction of other drivers as they come into view. That tactic is done to detect a surveillance. When faced with such a situation, the most appropriate course of action is to continue on in a normal manner while appropriately advising the second investigator, who can turn off the road and stop at some appropriate spot. When conditions permit, the lead vehicle will also turn off the road and stop. The investigators then sit and wait for the subject to reappear. It is important that the investigators wait for the subject at a location where their presence will not be obvious when the subject resumes travel and passes by. To accomplish this, it may be necessary for the second vehicle to turn around and go back a distance before such a location can be found. Similarly, it may be necessary for the lead vehicle to continue traveling ahead for some distance before stopping. The surveillance will resume once the subject resumes travel. The subject's new direction of travel will determine which investigator will take the lead position.

When two investigators using two vehicles are following a subject in relatively heavy traffic, it is generally necessary to stay relatively close to avoid losing the subject. In this endeavor it is usually desirable to stay in the subject's blind spot as much as possible, depending of course upon the circumstances. The second investigator should stay reasonably close to the first investigator, allowing perhaps one but not more than one unrelated vehicle to come between them. The positioning of the investigators' vehicles in relation to the subject should be frequently rotated.

Bumper Beepers

The difficult task of following a vehicle can be aided through the use of an electronic locating and tracking system, often referred to as a *bumper beeper*. Such a system consists of a miniature radio transmitter about the size of a pack of cigarettes or smaller, which is concealed on the undercarriage of a subject's vehicle (*see* Figures 4-13 and 4-14). The radio signal emitted by the beeper is received by a special radio receiver in the investigator's vehicle (*see* Figure 4-15). Some such receivers feature a direction-finding capability, while others do not. The one pictured does and is one of the most sophisticated systems available today.

Two distinct advantages are offered by a beeper system. The first is being able to follow a vehicle while remaining out of sight. The second benefit is being able to relocate a vehicle once it has been lost during a surveillance or to locate a vehicle at any time its whereabouts must be known. Beeper systems are especially useful for moving surveillance if a lone investigator must attempt to

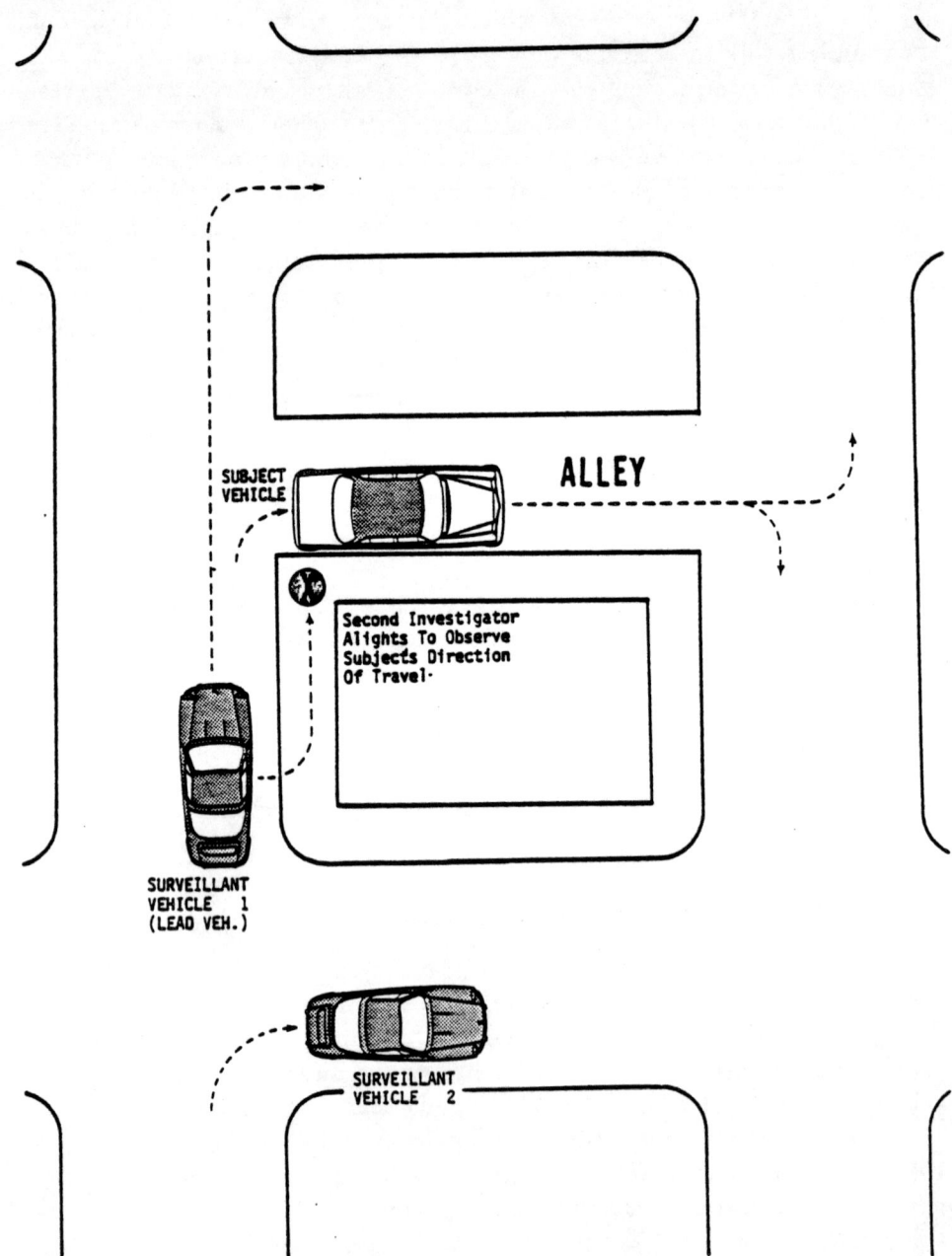

Figure 4-12. Subject turns into an alley. Lead vehicle (1) stops short of the alley, allowing an investigator to go on foot to see if the subject stops or passes through the alley and turns. If a turn is made, the direction of the turn is indicated. Vehicle (2) turned a block early. Either vehicle is in position to assume the lead, depending upon which way the subject may turn after passing through the alley.

follow a vehicle. This is very often the case with private investigators because of a client's unwillingness to pay the fee necessary for more than one investigator and vehicle.

The typical range of most beepers is anywhere from one to five miles on the open road when the receiver is in another vehicle. In a built-up urban area, the same beeper will have an effective range of only a few blocks to as little as a part of a block in some instances. The range will be better if the subject vehicle parks on a high parking ramp but may be lost entirely if an underground lot is used. Should the receiver be placed in an aircraft, the effective range can be increased from between one and five miles to well over twenty-five miles. Range is dependent upon the make and quality of the system being used.

RURAL SURVEILLANCE

General Considerations

Surveillance in rural areas will present some unique problems generally not encountered in the urban environment. Often, when attempting to follow a vehicle, the surveillant will not have other vehicles to blend with, and when at-

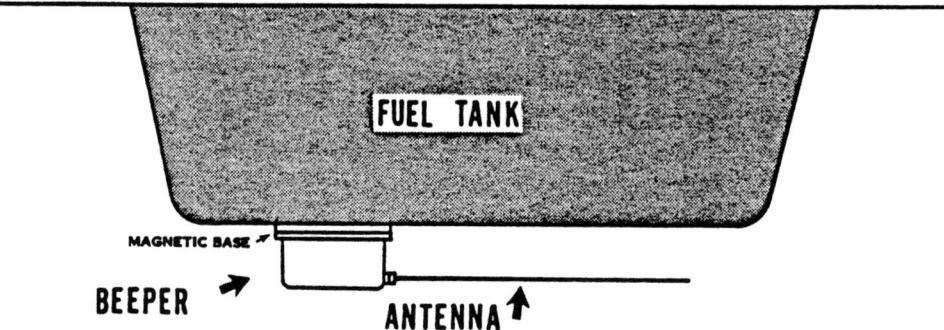

Figure 4-13. Beeper (radio transmitter) with magnetic base attached to the underside of a subject vehicle's gas tank. Antenna in the horizontal position shortens the effective transmitting range but reduces the chance of accidental discovery.

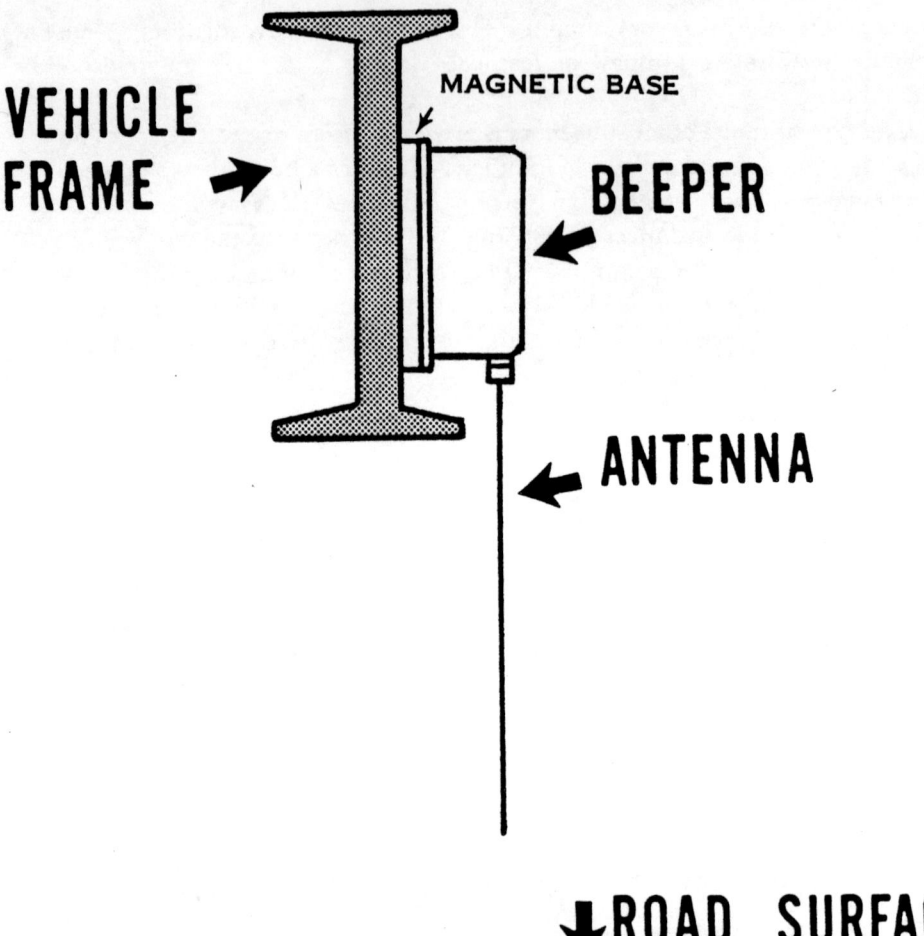

VEHICLE FRAME ➤

MAGNETIC BASE

BEEPER ⬅

⬅ **ANTENNA**

⬇**ROAD SURFACE**

Figure 4-14. Beeper may also be mounted to a vehicle frame. Here, the antenna in the vertical position offers greater range but is more likely to be noticed by a wary subject.

tempting stationary surveillance, the nature of the vantage point will differ considerably as well.

Although rural surveillance presents some unique difficulties that differ significantly from those encountered in the city, they are normally no more difficult to cope with if the investigator has an understanding of those techniques and methods appropriate to rural surveillance.

Not unlike an urban surveillance, the rural surveillance should be preceded by a preliminary survey of the area in which the surveillance is to be conducted or, at least, begun. The preliminary survey should take into consideration the

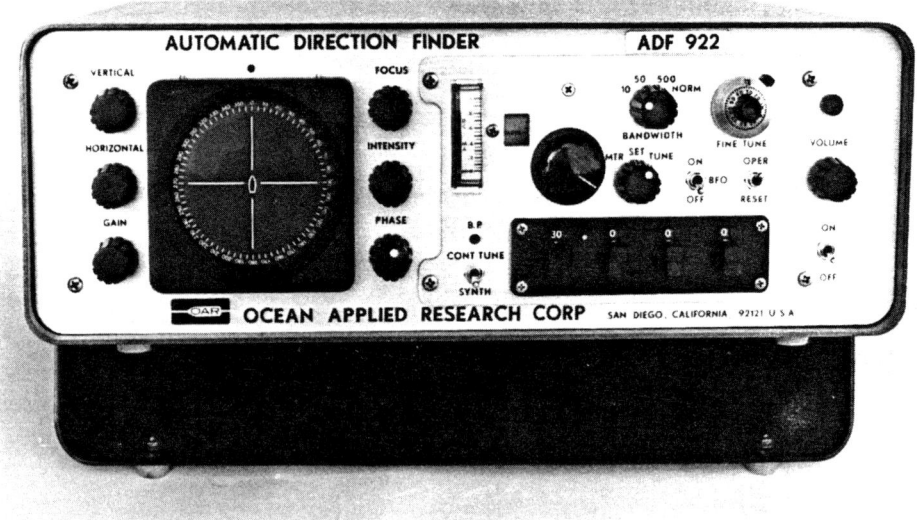

Figure 4-15. Special radio receiver indicates in degrees (see display at the left end of the instrument) the direction from which the beeper's signal is received. The typical range is one to five miles. (Courtesy of Ocean Applied Research Corporation)

road system for an area of perhaps five miles in all directions.

When selecting a rural vantage point, the investigator must consider a discreet means of traveling to and from the area. Additionally, the vantage point must provide suitable cover while at the same time affording an unobstructed view of the area to be surveilled. If the vantage point is being selected as a point from which to begin a vehicle surveillance, then it must also be such that from it the investigator can easily begin following the subject discreetly when travel begins. In some instances it will be necessary to have one investigator move in on foot with a two-way radio to observe the subject's area and then advise a second investigator when the subject begins moving and what the direction of his travel is.

Moving surveillance in the rural setting will generally require that a much greater distance be maintained between the vehicles. Only experience and good judgment can dictate just how much distance is appropriate in each instance. Vehicles used for rural surveillance should be of subtle colors. In many instances, allowing a cover of road dust to accumulate on the vehicle will prove advantageous.

In very sparsely populated rural areas, where following a subject without being observed would be difficult, the investigator may consider employing two or more radio-equipped surveillance vehicles (each a different color) to follow the subject, frequently rotating positions in relation to the subject. This *leapfrogging* is very effective inasmuch as the subject never sees the same vehicle following for any long period of time or for a very great distance.

In instances where it is believed that a very wary subject consistently travels the same route to the same destination at certain times, progressive surveillance, already discussed, may be in order.

When conducting stationary surveillance in a rural setting, a vehicle can sometimes be positioned for use as an observation post by utilizing foliage and distance for cover. In other instances, it will be necessary to move into the area on foot and, again, use foliage and distance for cover.

When conducting stationary surveillance in a rural setting, the investigator should consider wearing camouflage clothing. If such clothing is not available, then he should wear clothing of a color that will blend with the predominant color of the background against which it will be viewed.

When moving through a rural area on foot, every effort should be made to do so quietly, without being seen, and without leaving visual evidence, such as broken branches and trampled grass, of having been in the area. The best way to avoid being seen is to wear proper clothing, move slowly, be alert, and try to utilize natural cover such as that provided by natural contours in the land, trees, crops, and tall grass. Ridges should always be avoided, as they tend to silhouette the body against the sky.

To avoid problems with dogs and domestic livestock, the investigator should, in addition to moving slowly and quietly, move into the area from downwind or across-wind. If he is detected by curious animals, it is generally better to attempt to pacify them in some manner rather than to try to chase them away.

When working outdoors in rural areas, it is essential to make provisions for food, water, insect repellant if needed, and protective clothing for either exceptionally hot or cold climates.

VISION EXTENDERS

Because the distance between the investigator and the subject is generally quite great when conducting surveillance in both urban and rural areas, vision extenders such as binoculars and telescopes are essential. Also useful under certain circumstances are infrared scopes and the more recent and sophisticated electronic night vision devices. The latter instruments electronically amplify the existing level of illumination.

Binoculars are simply an optical device composed of two telescope systems mounted parallel to each other, enabling the user to view an enlarged image of some distant object using both eyes.

When considering the purchase of binoculars, there are five essential factors to be addressed. These include:

1. Magnifying power
2. Illumination (light-gathering capability)
3. Field of view
4. Weight
5. Durability

Aside from quality, binoculars differ primarily in —

1. Magnifying power,
2. Field of view, and
3. Illumination (light-gathering capability).

The specific binocular features that will best serve a particular investigator's needs will, of course, depend upon the intended use of the instrument. To be considered are such things as the subject matter, the distance, and the lighting conditions under which viewing will be accomplished. Long distances suggest need for a high magnifying power, while low light levels suggest the need for large aperture binoculars (large lens at the front of the instrument) that will gather greater quantities of light. A large aperture binocular, 7 × 50, for example, will gather much more light than will the unaided eye, making possible effective observations under light levels much too low for observation with the unaided eye.

Binoculars are generally identified by two numbers, such as 7 × 50 or 11 × 80. The first number indicates the magnifying power, while the second number indicates the diameter of the objective lens in millimeters. Hence, the 7 × 50 binocular is seven power with a fifty-millimeter diameter objective. To determine if binoculars are adequate for low-light observations, simply divide the diameter of the objective lens, fifty in this case, by the magnifying power, which in this example is seven: $50 \div 7 = 7.14$, which is the diameter of the shaft of light emitted by the eyepiece lens and approximates the diameter of the human eye when fully dilated.

Telescopes offer an advantage over binoculars in that they generally offer much greater degrees of magnification. The suitability for low-light viewing is determined the same way with a telescope as it is with binoculars. The diameter of the objective is divided by the magnifying power. For surveillance work, a telescope of moderate power will generally prove to be most useful; a twenty-power spotting scope will enable the investigator to read vehicle registration plates at distances approaching a half mile. Because of the greater magnifying power, a means to keep the instrument steady is essential.

Infrared viewers have been in existence since their introduction during the Second World War. These instruments function by illuminating the subject with a spotlight that is covered with a filter that allows the invisible infrared portion of the spectrum to pass but is opaque to visible light. The scope contains the necessary electronics to convert the invisible infrared image to a visible image for viewing purposes. The main advantage of the infrared scope over the more recently developed electronic light intensification equipment is lower cost to purchase.

Electronic light intensifiers operate by converting light energy to electrical energy, amplifying it, and then converting it back to light energy. Hence, they operate on the principle of light intensification. Unlike the infrared scope, which can be detected by a subject who also has such a scope, the electronic light intensifiers cannot be detected and are therefore referred to as *passive*. Generally, the illumination of weak starlight is sufficient to allow observations using such equipment, since the gain varies between 35,000 and over 65,000 times depending upon the equipment being used.

Chapter Five

SURVEILLANCE PHOTOGRAPHY

GENERAL CONSIDERATIONS

P HYSICAL surveillance often plays an important role in investigating cases such as illegal sales of contraband, in establishing and photographically documenting the activities of known and suspected criminals, and in disproving false claims of injuries. Because the camera, both still and motion picture, is such an invaluable tool to anyone engaged in surveillance, investigators should be proficient in the use of such equipment.

This chapter on surveillance photography, while offering the highlights of this unique application of photography, is not intended to offer more than that, for it is a very specialized area. There is, however, a book available that deals strictly and specifically with the topic of surveillance photography.*

To be effective at surveillance photography, the photographer must not only know his photographic equipment well, he must also be adept at physical surveillance. A word of caution is in order. When engaged in the covert photographing of a subject, the photographer must exercise extreme care not to violate that subject's right to privacy. To secure photographic evidence at the expense of violating the subject's rights will avail nothing if that violation will make the evidence inadmissible in a court of law.

CAMERA TYPES GENERALLY USED
FOR SURVEILLANCE PHOTOGRAPHY

As a general rule, the cameras best suited for surveillance photography are 35mm single lens reflex cameras, Super 8 and 16mm motion picture cameras, and in some unique situations, the subminiature cameras that are about the size of a pack of cigarettes or smaller.

---

*Siljander, Raymond P.: *Applied Surveillance Photography*. Springfield, Charles C Thomas Publisher, 1975.

65

The value of subminiature cameras lies primarily in their small size and easy concealment. The most notable advantage of 35mm single lens reflex cameras and 16mm motion picture cameras is their fast lenses and the wide variety of film types available for them. Super 8 motion picture cameras are preferred by many investigators because of their ease of operation and the relatively low cost and availability of film when on out-of-town assignments. However, there is a limited selection of film types available for Super 8 motion picture cameras. This can present problems when working under nighttime conditions where push processing of the film may be necessary.

TELEPHOTOGRAPHY

When engaged in surveillance photography, the photographer will find it is generally necessary to use a telephoto lens. Except for some distinct problems that are quite characteristic of telephoto photography, much of the art of telephotography is simply that of taking pictures. A telephoto lens working at f16 is very much like any other lens working at f16 insofar as exposure is concerned, the only exception being mirror lenses, which employ a system of mirrors to shorten the optical (light) path; with such lenses, there is a light loss of about two-thirds of an f-stop, which results because of a mirror's inability to reflect 100 percent of the light striking its surface.

The only distinguishing feature of a telephoto picture is a flat, long perspective. This is, however, a result of the long camera-to-subject distance and has nothing to do with the lens system being used. In the television showing of a baseball game, for example this compressed effect is quite apparent.

Because telephoto lenses tend to amplify any vibrations that may be present, firm support of both the camera body and the lens is essential. Figures 5-1 and 5-2 illustrate a couple of common methods of ensuring camera and lens stability. In addition, however, the photographer should exploit the advantages offered by a cable release. Figure 5-3 illustrates the results possible when using extreme telephoto lenses.

SURVEILLANCE PHOTOGRAPHY AT NIGHT
USING ULTRAHIGH-SPEED FILM

Very often, surveillance photography is needed at night. When this is the case, the surveillance photographer or investigator must decide between using ultrahigh-speed film and working with available light, using infrared materials, or using a night viewing device (NVD).

When working with ultrasound-speed film and available light, there is no easy way to ensure proper exposure. The photographer can, nonetheless, be

Figure 5-1. A belt pod is a useful aid when working with short to moderate telephoto lenses, still or motion picture.

Figure 5-2. Utilizing two tripods is often helpful in extreme telephoto work, and a cable release is also desirable. Shown is an 800mm f8 Vivitar® lens.

Figure 5-3. Subject photographed from a distance of 300 feet using (A) normal lens of 50mm, (B) 400mm telephoto lens, (C) 800mm telephoto lens, and (D) 2,000mm telephoto lens

C

assured of a very good chance of success by doing some experimental work, taking photographs of a person under various conditions so as to form an understanding of how best to approach various situations. He should try photographing a subject standing under a streetlight or photographing someone in a normally lit building from outside, as shown in Figure 5-4. He may also wish to attempt photographing a subject as the lights of a passing automobile pass over him briefly, being sure that the light source is a little bit in front of the subject so as to avoid a silhouette that will have little or no value for identification purposes.

Finally, when working at night with ultrahigh-speed film, it will generally be necessary to use as large an f-setting as possible and as slow a shutter speed as conditions will permit. The large f-setting will limit depth of field, and accurate focus is essential. The photographer should consider using an eyepiece magnifier; it will help ensure good focus. Because the shutter speed will be quite slow, proper support of the camera and lens is essential, or there will be image blur.

Figure 5-4. Night photograph of a subject in a normally lit building. Subject was photographed from about 150 feet using a 500mm f6.3 lens and an exposure duration of 1/30 second. Tri-X film® rated at E.I. 4000 (4000 ASA) was used.

PUSH PROCESSING PHOTOGRAPHIC FILM

As stated previously, the fast films and lenses of the 35mm still and the 16mm motion picture cameras are essential to the surveillance photographer. Unfortunately, these alone are often not enough, and the speed of the fastest film available, even when used with a very fast lens, is not sufficient to produce an acceptable negative under some sets of circumstances. The photographer can, in such cases, pretend the film is of an ASA rating much higher than it actually is and later compensate for the resultant underexposure by overdeveloping the film. For example, Tri-X® film, which is actually 400 ASA, may be exposed as if it were 1600 ASA. The film will naturally be underexposed as a result of this, and the photographer, realizing that fact, will compensate by overdeveloping the film. This is accomplished by increasing the development time, the development temperature, or both. This is called *push processing*. Although the quality of a negative that has been so processed will suffer from increased grain and contrast, the slight loss is inconsequential, considering that the push processing enabled the photographer to obtain a printable negative under conditions that would otherwise not have permitted it, and recognizing also that the use of a flash unit is out of the question in surveillance photography.

In Table 5-1 is a list of films and the recommended developing formulas for push processing them to various ASA ratings. The photographer should recognize that these development formulas are only recommended starting points, and the photographer should experiment a bit, as he may wish to adjust the times and temperatures to suit him and his specific needs best. This is especially true when pushing Tri-X film to 4000 ASA.

INFRARED SURVEILLANCE PHOTOGRAPHY

The Light Spectrum

The visible light spectrum is made up of various wavelengths of electromagnetic radiation. The spectrum is made up of violet light on one end, with a wavelength of about 400 millimicrons, then as the wavelengths get longer, blue, green, yellow, orange, and finally deep red, which is about 700 millimicrons. Beyond the two extremes is electromagnetic radiation, which continues to get shorter in wavelength on the violet and longer on the red end. Infrared photography takes place in the region just beyond the red end of the spectrum, between about 700 and 900 millimicrons. This region of the spectrum is not visible to the human eye. Although the spectrum does continue far beyond 900 millimicrons, it has nothing to do with infrared surveillance photography.

Table 5-I

FORMULAS FOR PUSH-PROCESSING PHOTOGRAPHIC FILMS

Kodak Tri-X® film. Agitate at sixty-second intervals.

	400 ASA	Normal development
E.I.	800 ASA	D-76, 12 min. at 68°F.
E.I.	1200 ASA	D-76, 9¾ min. at 75°F. or HC-110 (dil. A), 6½ min. at 68°F. or Acufine® developer, 5¼ min. at 68°F.
E.I.	1600 ASA	D-76, 13 min. at 75°F. or HC-110 (dil. A), 8 min. at 68°F.
E.I.	2400 ASA	Diafine®, two-step development process, see instructions on package.
E.I.	4000 ASA	HC-110 replenisher, 1:15 (one part replenisher to 15 parts water). Develop for 8 min. at 75°F. Agitate at 3 and 6 min. Discard at 8 min. *The photographer should experiment a bit as he may wish to alter development times and the agitation intervals to suit individual needs and techniques.*

Kodak 2475 High-Speed Recording® film.

E.I.	4000 ASA	DK-50, 9 min. at 68°F.
E.I.	6400 ASA	Diafine, mix solutions A & B at 70°F.
		Develop in solution A for 3 min. and then in solution B for 3 min., rinse well in running water for 1 min. at about 70°F. and redevelop 2 min. in both solutions A & B. Rinse, fix, and dry.

Kodak High Speed Ektachrome® film.

Follow instructions provided with E-4 chemicals.

Extend first development times only.	(Daylight)	(Tungsten)
Normal Development	160 ASA	125 ASA
Normal plus 35% increase	E.I. 320 ASA	E.I. 250 ASA
Normal plus 75% increase	E.I. 640 ASA	E.I. 500 ASA

Kodak Ektachrome-X® film.

Follow instructions provided with E-4 chemicals.

Extend first development time only.		
Normal Development	64 ASA	
Normal plus 35% increase	E.I. 125 ASA	
Normal plus 75% increase	E.I. 250 ASA	

Note: The above formulas are general guides and may be altered some to better suit individual needs and techniques. This holds true especially for Tri-X film rated at E.I. 4000 ASA.

Basic Technique

Basically, all the investigator needs to surreptitiously take an infrared photograph of someone in the dark is any 35mm camera, a roll of Kodak High-Speed Infrared® film, a gelatin Kodak Wratten Filter Number 87®, and an electronic strobe unit. The higher the BCPS (candlepower) rating of the strobe, the better. The film is a special film that is sensitive to a range of electromagnetic radiation between 700 and 900 millimicrons. Unfortunately, this film is also sensitive to the visible region of the spectrum.

To utilize the equipment that has just been outlined, the investigator need only place the film into the camera. This must be done in total darkness because the cassette will not block the infrared radiation as it does the visible light. A change bag is handy for this purpose. Next, the infrared filter is placed over the strobe unit. Electrician's tape and a small rectangular piece of glass will work well for this purpose. Infrared film is sensitive and will respond to visible light just as it will to infrared radiation, but there is no need to place a filter over the lens because the photographing will take place in darkness. Lights in the vicinity, such as streetlights, will present no problem. The filter over the strobe unit is necessary so that the subject does not detect the flash when he is photographed.

Once the camera assembly has been made ready, it will be necessary to establish a guide number so that proper exposure can be determined for various camera-to-subject distances. This is easily accomplished by taking a subject at a known distance (twenty feet, for example) and photographing that subject at all f-settings. After being developed, the film is examined, and the f-setting that gave the best exposure is multiplied by the camera-to-subject distance. For example, if the camera-to-subject distance was twenty feet and it is found that f4 gave the most correct exposure, then eighty is the guide number to be used with that film type, strobe, and filter ($4 \times 20 = 80$). In the future, the correct exposure is determined by dividing eighty by the camera-to-subject distance: the answer will be the proper f-setting to use.

In infrared photography, it is necessary to make an adjustment in focus because when properly focused for a visual image, the lens will *not* be properly focused for an infrared image. This correction is made by extending the lens from the film plane by .25 percent of the focal length of the lens being used. Most lenses made for 35mm cameras have an indicator mark on the lens to aid the photographer in this task.

The technique that has been discussed will offer a camera-to-subject distance of about fifty feet. There is a method of using a fresnel lens to make a telephoto strobe out of a normal strobe unit, which makes it possible to photograph subjects in detail in the 200-foot range. That is discussed in detail in the book, *Applied Surveillance Photography*. Also discussed in that book is infrared motion picture photography. Figure 5-5 is a typical infrared photograph.

PHOTOGRAPHY AT NIGHT
USING STARLIGHT SCOPES

Starlight scopes are a modern and more sophisticated version of the famous World War II snooperscopes. Starlight scopes differ from snooperscopes

Figure 5-5. Subject photographed at 100 feet in total visual darkness using infrared materials and a 500mm f6.3 lens.

mainly in that they operate on the principle of light intensification rather than on infrared radiation, which is the case with infrared snooperscopes. Generally, one star will provide sufficient illumination for a starlight scope to function satisfactorily, and that is where the term comes from. Basically, the light intensification is accomplished by taking light energy, changing it to electrical energy, amplifying it, and then changing it back to light energy. The image produced is a greenish white.

Most manufacturers and distributors of starlight scopes offer adapters by which cameras may be attached to their units for night photography. Among the cameras that may successfully be adapted to a starlight scope are most 35mm single lens reflex models, motion picture cameras, and video cameras (*see* Figures 5-6, and 5-7).

Figure 5-6. 35mm single lens reflex camera coupled, by means of a relay lens, to a Smith and Wesson Star-tron MK 222® with an 85mm, f1.8 lens. (Courtesy of Smith and Wesson)

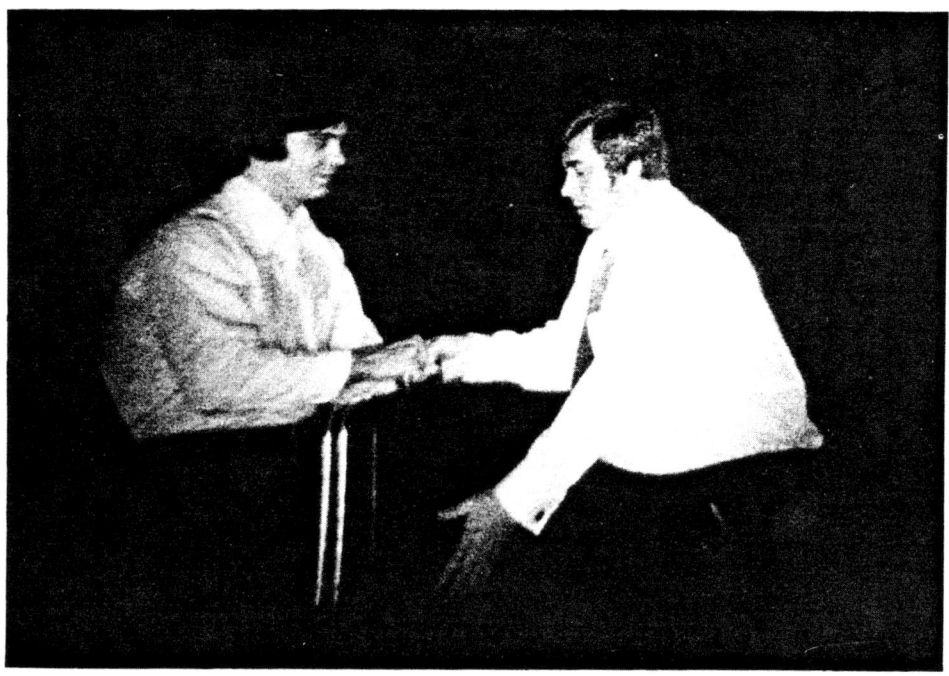

Figure 5-7. Subjects were photographed through a Star-tron at a distance of about eighty feet using Kodak 2475® high-speed recording film rated at E.I. 1000 (1000 ASA). Exposure was 1/20 second with an illumination level approximating normal starlight conditions. (Courtesy of Smith and Wesson)

Chapter Six

SOURCES OF INFORMATION

T HE average person generally has but little appreciation and awareness of the many records and documents each person leaves behind as he or she goes through life. Such records provide a testimony of each person's having lived and died, as well as of most of what was done between those two events. When used properly, such records can provide the private investigator with a vast amount of information.

Just a few of the many records and documents a person creates going through life are the *birth certificate,* which is filed with the health department when the individual is born and lists when and where the person was born and who the parents were, and records of any *medical* attention received in life. When a person enters and goes through school, there are again records created. There may be additional information recorded with trade or professional associations, as well as with license bureaus, when and if the person obtains a license for any purpose such as certain businesses and driving. When the person marries, there is again a record made of both the applicant and the license, reflecting such information as who is being married, when, where, and by whom, and also the identity of the spouse's parents and where they are from. In the event the marriage proves to be unsuccessful, there will be a rather revealing record in divorce court available for all to see. In the event a death has occurred in the family, there may be probate court records that will reflect a great deal of information. All other court judgments and convictions can also create revealing records. Additionally there are employment records to be considered, as well as credit records in the event the person has applied for credit. Also, property tax assessment records are available to show what property a person owns.

There is a tremendous amount of information available on any given person and that person's activities. Such information can provide the basis for many investigations. However, the many records mentioned in this example include both public records that are available to anyone and confidential records that are accessible only through the cooperation of an informant. The investigator should also recognize that some records are available at no cost while others require a fee. Similarly, some types of information may be obtained over the telephone, while others must be obtained in person. It should also be understood that records which are considered public in some areas may be considered confidential in others.

When using records and documents in an effort to obtain information, the investigator should be sure to use first those sources which are easily accessible and most likely to produce the desired results and save for last the sources that are more difficult to use and less likely to provide the desired information.

Records that are available from city, county, state, and federal governmental agencies vary somewhat depending to a large degree upon the way the individual governmental agencies are structured in a given area. The investigator must check his area of operation to establish exactly what is available and the procedure by which it can be obtained. In researching what may and may not be readily available through city, county, state, and federal agencies in a particular area, the telephone directory (white pages) is the most readily available and convenient source to use. A little research either by telephone to or in person at these different agencies can be very rewarding.

The following lists of records found on the local, county, state, and federal levels is by no means all of the types of records maintained on these levels but includes those an investigator will use most often.

MUNICIPAL OR CITY RECORDS

Every city in the nation maintains a number of records regarding the people who live there and the functions that take place within its boundaries. Some of the typical departments within a city and the records kept there are listed in Table 6-I. When reviewing this list, the investigator should remember that the names of these departments are only examples and that these departments may not be called by the same name in each city. Also, the information in each department may vary from city to city.

COUNTY RECORDS

Like the cities, each county within each state maintains some records on its citizens and the activities that go on within its boundaries. In some cases the functions of a county office and a city office might actually overlap somewhat or at least appear to overlap. It will take some research on the investigator's part to sort out these overlaps and find exactly what records are maintained in each department. For example, many times a business that has to have a city

Table 6-I

MUNICIPAL OR CITY DEPARTMENTS

AND THEIR AREAS OF RESPONSIBILITY

DEPARTMENT NAME	RESPONSIBLE FOR
Business Licenses Department or Departments of Weights and Measures	control and issue of licenses to many different types of business that are required to have a license to operate (In many smaller cities, licenses are issued by the city finance department, city clerk's office, city treasurer, or even the police department.)
Building Safety Department	building permits for any construction that is to be done within the city limits
City Courts	records on all civil and criminal proceedings that happen to fall within its jurisdiction
Airport or Aviation Department	records on the operation of all city-owned airports
Fire Department	records on all fires reported within the city plus records on fire safety inspections and burning permits
Health Department	establishment and enforcement of city health regulations such as seeing that restaurants maintain an acceptable level of cleanliness
Police Department	all police matters within the city boundaries
Municipal or Justice Courts	all local misdemeanor crimes
Board of Education	administration of all public schools
Truant Officer	handling problems with delinquent students (works for school district)

business license to operate within a particular city will find that it is also necessary to have another license from the county. Generally, there is a broader range of services provided on a county level, and these records are the ones most often used. Some of the most often used county record sources can be found in Table 6-II. As stated previously about city records, the names shown for each department may vary from county to county, and the information contained in these departments can vary widely depending upon each county's decisions on how to handle its affairs.

STATE RECORDS

As with cities and counties, each state operates a wide variety of record-keeping departments. Some of these departments, again, cover areas that overlap areas of record maintenance on the city and county levels, but most of the

Table 6-II

COUNTY DEPARTMENTS AND THEIR AREAS OF RESPONSIBILITY

DEPARTMENT NAME	RESPONSIBLE FOR
Tax Assessor's Office	records on such things as real estate taxes, personal property taxes, etc. (This is a highly used source of information and can be especially helpful in locating a person or determining a person's assets.)
County Recorder's Office, Registrar of Deeds, or Recorder of Deeds	records on such things as chattel mortages and liens and many other important documents (Many individuals records and important papers, such as military discharges, financial statements, and credit records, are recorded with this office. Also, vital statistics are maintained here, the records of all births, deaths, and marriages that occur within the county.)
Coroner's Office	establishing the cause of death in cases where death may have occurred under unusual or questionable circumstances keeping death certificates on all deaths that occur within the county. (This department may also establish and maintain health standards within the county.)
Superior Court	all civil and criminal proceedings that occur within its jurisdiction
Sheriff's Department	law enforcement services within the county (Usually the Sheriff's Department does not operate within city boundaries unless requested to do so by the city.)

time this is not the case. Sometimes to gain access to state records it is necessary to obtain them from the state capital, which may make it necessary to either write for the information or actually go there in person. Other times, however, a branch location of a state agency or department can obtain the information the investigator is looking for even though the information originated in a different part of the state. This is where advanced research will pay off. Information, for example, on a driver's license or on a motor vehicle's registration can sometimes be obtained statewide through a local branch of the state's motor vehicle department. Many times the same information can also be obtained through the mail. There is a set procedure to go through in both cases, and a small fee is also customary. Table 6-III shows a few of the more common state governmental agencies and departments and the type of information they might be expected to contain.

FEDERAL RECORDS

As a general rule, federal records are harder to obtain access to than those on the city, county, and state levels. Part of the difficulty stems from the fact

Table 6-III

STATE DEPARTMENTS AND THEIR AREAS OF RESPONSIBILITY

DEPARTMENT NAME	RESPONSIBLE FOR
Alcoholic Beverage Control Department	issuing licenses and enforcing state liquor laws
State Police, Highway Patrol or Department of Public Safety (state law enforcement division)	enforcement of highway traffic laws and other state laws such as those on drug possession (This department also may provide for a fire marshal's office and investigative and laboratory facilities for smaller local police agencies who cannot afford these facilities. They also usually provide for a statewide pool of criminal information.)
Corporations Commission	up-to-date records on all businesses that are incorporated and operating within the state's boundaries
Highway Department	up-to-date records on all motor vehicle accidents that occur within the state
Department of Motor Vehicle and Driver's Licensing Department	records of all motor vehicles and all licensed drivers with the state (This department also keeps records on all traffic law violation convictions and records on lien holders of vehicles registered in the state.)
Secretary of State and the State Attorney General's Office	a very wide variety of services, which vary greatly from state to state (The investigator should contact these two offices in the state or states in which he intends to work and find out what is available.)
Professional and Trade Licensing Bureaus	maintaining records on a large variety of professions and trades that they license
Industrial Accident Commission, Workmen's Compensation Division	all workmen's on-the-job injuries that occur within the state
State Correctional Institutions	state prison system, which is responsible for the handling of all those convicted of crimes against the state and sentenced to serve time
Bureau of Vital Statistics	statewide central records of marriage, divorce, birth, and death
State Game Warden	enforcement of hunting and fishing laws and issuing of licenses

that their offices handle large geographical areas, and so finding the department that has the information desired is not always the easiest thing to do. Once access has been obtained, however, these records can be very beneficial. Table 6-IV gives a few examples of what some federal records contain.

Table 6-IV

FEDERAL DEPARTMENTS AND THEIR AREAS OF RESPONSIBILITY

DEPARTMENT NAME	RESPONSIBLE FOR
U.S. District Court	all proceedings conducted within its jurisdiction. (This court also maintains federal bankruptcy filing records.)
Federal Aviation Administration	registration of all federally licensed aircraft as well as the certificates of all licensed pilots, and their medical certificates (Records of any official suspension or revocation of pilot privileges as well as all liens on federally licensed aircraft are also maintained in the Oklahoma City office.)
U.S. Postal Service	forwarding addresses, which can be obtained from the branch office that served the last known address of the party being sought (If the investigator wants the address right away he can go in person, pay a small fee, and get the address, or he can send a letter to the last known address with the written instruction "Do not forward, address correction requested" on the envelope. He should be sure to include a return address, for obvious reasons. The letter will be returned with the new address.)
Department of Justice	
Bureau of Narcotics and Dangerous Drugs	enforcement of drug laws (This department also assists local and state agencies as requested.)
Federal Bureau of Investigation	investigation of all crimes against the federal government (This department also assists local and state law enforcement agencies as requested.)
Immigration and Naturalization Service	records on all aliens entering the country legally and acquiring U.S. citizenship
Department of the Treasury	
Alcohol, Tobacco, and Firearms Division	enforcement of alcohol and tobacco taxes and firearms laws, registration of automatic weapons, and investigation of bomb-threat cases
Coast Guard	investigation of all offshore smuggling matters
Internal Revenue Service	enforcement of federal income tax matters
Secret Service	protection of the president and dignitaries, tracking down counterfeiting operations
Nuclear Regulatory Commission (formerly the Atomic Energy Commission)	all nuclear materials
Federal Communications Commission	regulation of all radio transmissions, issuance of radio licenses, and investigation of violations
Interstate Commerce Commission	regulation of all interstate shipments of goods, licensing of truck lines, and overseeing of the railroads
Federal Trade Commission	investigating charges of false advertising and regulating trade practices
Securities and Exchange Commission	regulating the stock market and overseeing sales of securities
Veterans Administration	operation of military hospitals, and has records on ex-military personnel who have been treated in military hospitals

CONFIDENTIAL RECORDS

No attempt was made to try to identify most of the sources referred to previously as to whether or not the records each source contained were open to the public. The federal government sets one policy that applies to all of its branches similarly. For example, the policy on forwarding addresses applies to every branch of the U.S. Postal Service throughout the country. If the investigator contacts a particular federal agency in California and it will allow access to its records, the same agency in any other part of the country will also allow review of its records. If particular records are confidential in one place, they are confidential everywhere.

This is not true in dealing with city, county, and state governmental agencies, however. All court proceedings are of course open to the public unless the records have been sealed for some special reason, but many other governmental record sources will vary from open to the public to confidential, based on whatever that particular city, county, or state decides it wants to do. It will be up to the investigator to research this wherever he will be working.

Reference was made to confidential records, records that are not open to the public. In some cases the government has decided that for some reason the records should only be viewed by certain authorized persons. Classified military documents, for example, fall into this category. Federal law states that only people possessing the proper clearance and "need to know" can have access to these records. It should go without saying that if a governmental agency restricts access to its records, the private investigator must honor this restriction. To ignore the restriction and attempt to gain access anyway could be legally disastrous. At the very least he would be risking loss of license.

There are many records, however, that are not actually illegal to see but that have been restricted by a departmental policy limiting view to certain people only. The records at most private businesses, for example, are considered confidential since they are not open to the public's view. Where private industry is involved or where the violation of a law is not involved, however, the investigator can many times gain access to supposedly confidential records through a carefully cultivated informant.

An *informant* is a person who has access to some information that the investigator is in need of and who will provide the information in exchange for something. For example, say a large manufacturing firm has established a policy of giving out only very limited information regarding its employees. A private investigator interested in gaining more specific information regarding a particular employee certainly could not simply go into the company and get the information from the person's personnel file. He could, however, get the desired information from an employee of the company who either had access to the personnel file or knew what it was the investigator desired to learn. The person providing the information would be considered an informant. The informant would help because he was offered money or simply because he wanted to be helpful.

All good investigators attempt to develop informants whenever the opportunity arises. How to go about developing an informant has to be a personal matter. Most of the time an informant is developed strictly on a personal basis of friendship. Sometimes an informant will agree to provide information for a fee, and on occasion these people have been known even to search out private investigators to sell their information to. A private investigator's "stock in trade" is information, so the more reliable information he has access to, the better his eventual results will be.

In discussing informants, it is important to reemphasize one point mentioned earlier and add one more caution. An investigator must be careful not to induce someone to break the law to obtain information, and he must protect the identity of all informants. If someone provides information in a confidential manner, the investigator must be sure not to identify the source, not even to the client. He may need such information again someday.

LISTINGS OF BIRTH, MARRIAGE, DIVORCE, AND DEATH RECORDS

Many times, in conducting various types of investigations, the investigator will find it necessary to obtain a record of a birth, death, marriage, or divorce. These records can usually be obtained simply by writing to the agency responsible for maintaining them. Many times there is one central source located within a particular state or territory. Other times it will be necessary to contact the individual city or county involved.

All of the records will have to be purchased with a small fee, which will vary from area to area and will have to be included with the written request for the record desired. The investigator can either call ahead and determine the exact cost of the record or send $3 or $4 along with the request. (Usually an overpayment will be returned with the information requested, if available, but the fee will not usually be returned if the record is unavailable, since the fee usually includes the cost for the search of the records.)

When writing for a copy of a particular record, the investigator should furnish as much information as possible to help ensure that the record can be located. Often there may be two or more records on individuals with names that are similar or even exactly the same. In cases like this the records searcher will usually advise that more information is necessary and another fee will have to be paid; that only delays obtaining the information.

When seeking a record, the investigator should keep in mind that births occurring before birth registration was required or births not registered when they occurred may have been filed as "delayed birth registrations" or may not be on file at all. He should also bear in mind that all of these records are generally maintained alphabetically by year. Most places will charge a fee for each year that they have to search, so he should at least try to narrow the search as much as possible by having an approximate date of when the marriage, divorce, birth, or death occurred.

When writing for marriage records, the investigator should try to include as much of the following as possible:

1. Full name of bride and groom (including nicknames)
2. Residence addresses at time of marriage
3. Ages at time of marriage (or dates of birth)
4. Date and place of marriage
5. Purpose for which copy is needed
6. Relationship to person whose record is on file

When writing for divorce records, he should try to include as much of the following as possible:

1. Full name of husband and wife (including nicknames)
2. Present residence address
3. Former addresses (as in court records)
4. Ages at time of divorce (or dates of birth)
5. Date and place of divorce or annulment of marriage
6. Type of final decree
7. Purpose for which copy is needed
8. Relationship to persons whose record is on file

When writing for birth or death records, the investigator should try to include as much of the following as possible:

1. Full name of the person whose record is being requested
2. Sex and race
3. Parent's names, including maiden name of mother
4. Month, day, and year of the birth or death
5. Place of birth or death (city or town, county and state, and name of hospital, if any)
6. Purpose for which copy is needed
7. Relationship to person whose record is being requested

DIRECTORIES

To the investigator, directories can be a valuable source of *lead information*.

However, they should not be considered as a final authority. Any information obtained from them should be verified before it is reported to a client. When considering the reliability of information obtained from directories, the investigator should bear in mind the time lapses between the time information is obtained and the directory actually appears in print. In some instances a new directory, just released, contains information that is already several months old. Also, some directories are only published once every few years. Due to the fact that people die, move, change affiliations, etc., the average directory has between 15 and 40 percent changes each year. The national average of directory changes is approximately 25 percent each year. That illustrates the importance of investigator's using the most current directory available and then verifying the information before reporting it to clients.

Realizing the limitations of directories and using them for what they are, the investigator will find that they contain a wealth of information. A trip to the public library will reveal a number of directories on an extremely wide variety of topics. One or more directories can be found in almost any area in which a person might be interested. Some typical directories cover topics such as trade associations, professional associations, manufacturing firms, lawyers, doctors, bankers and their institutions, education, real estate, agriculture, sports and recreational facilities, and others too numerous to name. There is even a directory of directories, which is in itself a very sizable volume.

The directories that will be discussed here are only a few of the more frequently used ones, and this is by no means a complete listing of all of the directories that an investigator might want to use. The easiest and cheapest way to utilize directories is to go to the public library and find out ahead of time what is available. The investigator may eventually find that certain frequently used directories would be desirable to own, and he can then purchase those separately.

Telephone Directories

Any discussion of directories should begin with the single most often used and many times overlooked directory available to the investigator, which is the telephone directory. All too often an investigator will spend a great deal of time examining a variety of sources when the needed information was available all the while right in the telephone directory. Each investigator should maintain a complete selection of telephone directories for the area in which he expects to conduct his business. Such a set may even include directories for all major cities nationwide, if he desires and the storage space is available.

Most people are not aware that they may obtain, through the telephone company and at no cost or very little cost to themselves, directories for as many cities as they desire. When requesting directories from the telephone company the investigator must advise them that the directories will be used for placing long-distance calls. In updating his telephone directory library each year, he should retain as many of the old directories as space will allow. These old directories can prove useful in helping to establish such things as prior residency when doing a background investigation on an individual. If space does not allow the investigator to build up his own set of old directories, then he can utilize the resources of the telephone company, since they do maintain a library of old directories for the area that each branch serves.

City Directories

The next most often used directory is the city directory. The city directory is published in each city of less than one million population. Most of the city directories are published by R.L. Polk and Company, although there are some published by other companies. Generally speaking, all of the city directories follow the same format: They contain the name, occupation, and sometimes place of employment of each adult resident of the city. This directory will also reflect the first name of nonemployed spouses. In the back of the directory is a householder's guide. In this section are names of streets listed alphabetically and houses listed numerically, opposite which are the names of the respective householders and a symbol indicating whether the householder owns the home.

The city directory can have many uses for the private investigator. It can be helpful in locating missing persons or in providing the names of neighbors to be contacted when conducting a background investigation or insurance investigation, for example. If a city directory is readily available, it could become a good habit to check it each time an investigation is commenced: It may serve as a double check to make sure the subject's name is spelled correctly or the address is written down correctly. That in itself can be an enormous time-saver, as anyone who has attempted to do a background investigation on a person whose name or address was given to them incorrectly will attest.

Catalog of City, County, and State Directories
Published in North America

This directory is published by the Association of North American Directory Publishers, 270 Orange Street, New Haven, Connecticut, and covers the approximately fifty publishers of city, county, and state directories and the several hundred directories these publishers issue each year. This directory provides the name, address, and telephone number of each publisher indexed by the directories they publish. This is useful when considering the purchase of one or more of these directories for personal use. This directory also lists many additional things such as auto ownership, census figures, and farmers.

Guide to American Directories

This directory, which has become known as the "Directory of Directories," published by B. Klein Publications, Inc., Coral Springs, Florida, and Rye, New York, is a guide to the major business directories covering all of the major industrial, professional, and mercantile categories. This source lists the major directories published by business and reference book publishers, magazines, trade associations, chambers of commerce, and city, state, and federal governmental agencies.

Directory Information Service

This is another "Directory of Directories," published by Information Enterprises and distributed by Gale Research Company, Detroit, Michigan. It lists approximately 1,800 current directories, covering a similar scope as the *Guide to American Directories*, although not with as many listings.

Cross Street Directory

There are several publishers of this type of directory, and all are based on the telephone directory. This directory takes the alphabetical listings of the telephone directory and cross references them in two different ways, by street address and also by telephone number. The street address section lists everyone in the telephone directory by street address. The streets are arranged alphabetically, and then everyone on that street with a listed telephone is shown by address, listed in numerical order. The individual resident is listed after the address, with the telephone number following. Using this portion of the directory, the investigator can determine who lives at a particular address on any street. He can also find out the names of that person's neighbors, if interested.

The other major section of this directory contains telephone numbers listed in numerical order, with the resident's name and address following. Using this portion of the directory, the investigator can find out who has a particular telephone number even if all he knows is that number. Additionally, in this directory after the various listings usually will be found symbols that can indicate the length of time the party has resided at the address in question or if their's is a new listing. There is generally a section that indicates the price range of the residences within each given section of the city. Apartment complexes and office buildings show all of the tenants therein listed together.

Standard and Poor's Register of Corporations, Directors, and Executives

Published by Standard and Poor's Corporation, 345 Hudson Street, New

York, N.Y., this is a listing of approximately 40,000 officials of various firms. Also included are biographies of approximately 75,000 directors and executives. The companies' name, address, and telephone numbers are listed, as are the principal executives, number of employees, financial data, trade and brand names, and products or services offered.

MaCrae's Blue Book

Published by MaCrae's Blue Book Company, 100 Shore Drive, Hinsdale, Illinois, this directory lists alphabetically U.S. manufacturing firms. Given also are products manufactured, trade names, and catalogs of advertisers.

National Directory of Addresses and Telephone Numbers

This directory is published by Bantam Books, 666 Fifth Avenue, New York, N.Y., and includes 50,000 business firms (doing in excess of $10 million in annual sales), governmental offices, banks, hotels, consulates and embassies, colleges and universities, newspapers, radio and television stations, race tracks, and bail bondsmen. Listed are these establishment's names, addresses, and telephone numbers.

World Wide Business Publications Directory

Simon and Schuster, Inc., 1 West 39th Street, New York, N.Y., publishes this directory, which contains information on how to obtain any of 6,000 business, trade, or professional publications published throughout the world.

The Martindale-Hubbell Law Directory

This source lists all practicing attorneys by city and state, including lawyers in principal cities throughout the world. Included is such data as date of birth, education, admission date, and some financial ratings. Also, the directory contains digests of laws in every state and all U.S. possessions, plus Canada and some other foreign countries.

American Medical Directory

Published by the American Medical Association, this directory lists approximately 365,000 medically qualified physicians in the United States and U.S. possessions. Included with these listings is such information as a physician's professional address, medical education, specialty areas and membership in national scientific medical societies.

Rand-McNally International Banker's Directory

Some 40,000 banks and branches are indexed, as well as the names of officers and certain other employees. Listings also include statement figures and correspondents.

International Directory of Detective Agencies

Published by Inter-State Service Company, Inc., Neosho, Missouri, this directory lists 500 American and foreign detective agencies.

Society of Professional Investigators, Inc. Roster

This is a publication of the Society of Professional Investigators, Inc., P.O. Box 1197, Church Street Station, New York, N.Y. Listed are the current members of the Society. Included also are many of the top law enforcement investigative detectives, special agents, and heads of law enforcement agencies from around the country.

Who's Who Directories

There are a large number of "Who's Who" directories put out by several different publishers. These directories put together large groups of prominent or noteworthy individuals in general or specific areas such as the fields of business, finance, politics, art, insurance, etc. All include biographical information on the people selected for their respective publications.

These are only a very few of the many and varied directories available. The investigator need only take time to find them and determine what kind of information they possess. If used properly they can many times supply the right lead to help bring a case to a successful conclusion. However, they are not a final solution to problems and should not be used as if they were.

INFORMATION TYPES AND SOURCES CROSS-INDEXED

Information Sought	Sources Where It Can Be Found
Addresses — business or residential	Telephone directory, city directory, voter's registration or registrar of voters office, criss-cross directory
Attorneys	*The Martindale-Hubbell Law Directory*, telephone directory — yellow pages, state bar registry, state lawyers' manual

Automobiles — ownership and liens	state department of motor vehicles
Autopsy report	City or county clerk, city or county court, city health department, or bureau of vital statistics
Banks, officers, or cashiers	*Rand-McNally International Bankers Directory*
Bankruptcy information	U.S. district court, credit bureau files (occasionally)
Births, deaths, marriages, and divorces	City or county clerk, city or county court house, bureau of vital statistics, city health department
Brand names and trademarks	*MaCrae's Blue Book, Standard and Poor's Register of Corporations*
Business reputation	Local better business bureau, trade associations, other local businesses
Civil litigation	U.S. district courthouse, superior or municipal courts, justice of the peace, credit bureaus
Corporations and their officers or executives	State corporations commissioner, county courthouse in county of home office, Dun and Bradstreet, *Standard and Poor's Register of Corporations*
Deeds	City or county clerk, county courthouse, recorder of deeds
Criminal records	U.S. district court, local or state police department, county sheriff's department, superior or municipal court records
Doctors	*American Medical Directory*, county medical association directory, telephone directory — yellow pages
Financial	Dun and Bradstreet, credit bureaus, county court, and recorder's office
Fires	Local fire department
Liens or mortgages	Recorder of deeds, county court records
Maps, townships	county surveyor's office
Military discharges	Registrar of deeds, county courthouse
Manufacturing firms	*MaCrae's Blue Book*, local chamber of

	commerce
Property — personal and real	County tax assessor's office, local credit bureau
Reputation — personal	Present and former neighbors, present and former work associates, newspaper clipping library

SOCIAL SECURITY NUMBERS

All persons working legally in the United States are required to register with the Social Security Administration. The Social Security Administration issues all persons a social security number, which stays with them for life. Each state issues social security cards and numbers beginning with a specific three-digit series. By knowing a person's social security number and referring to the chart in Appendix B, the investigator can determine the state that first issued that number. This can be especially helpful in conducting a background investigation on a person beginning with limited information. It can also be useful in trying to locate a missing person.

Chapter Seven

PRETEXT INVESTIGATIONS

GENERAL CONSIDERATIONS

THE private investigator, unlike police and governmental investigators, has no legal authority above and beyond that enjoyed by the average citizen. Because of the nature of the work generally done by private investigators, they frequently find it necessary to obtain information from people who would not normally be willing to divulge information should they be approached in an open and direct manner. Similarly, private investigators are often faced with the necessity of obtaining entrance, for observation purposes, to someone's home or to a business or industrial firm such as a factory or warehouse, an entrance that would be denied were the true purpose and identity of the investigator known. It is for this reason that private investigators, unlike police or governmental investigators, have out of necessity become proficient in the art of conducting pretext investigations.

LEGAL CONSIDERATIONS

The investigator engaged in pretext work will find it necessary, because of the very nature of pretext work, to use names and supposed associations that are fictitious in every respect. To avoid legal difficulties, however, the investigator must never represent himself as being a law enforcement officer from either a municipal, county, state, or federal agency or as being a representative of an existing firm or company. Similarly, the investigator must avoid using a name that so closely resembles that of an existing firm, company, or agency as to mislead the subject of his pretext work into believing that he is in fact associated with a genuine concern.

When engaged in pretext work, the investigator should be aware of things that could result in a civil lawsuit. If a plaintiff or a defendant in a civil suit is being represented by legal counsel, the investigator should be aware of the problems that could result should he make contact with that individual under pretext. If an investigator makes contact with a person under such circumstances, he runs the risk of being sued for invasion of privacy should his identity and purpose be discovered and proven.

For this reason, it is important that the investigator take reasonable safeguards in keeping with the hazards of a particular investigation. Experience has shown that when conducting a pretext investigation in a neighborhood environment, a female investigator generally encounters less resistance. Thus it would be well worth considering using a female to conduct a neighborhood pretext unless the particular circumstances favor a male investigator. People are generally less apt to associate a female with work of a clandestine nature.

PITFALLS

Some common pitfalls to be avoided when conducting pretext investigations include the following:

1. The subject who has been burned by a previous investigation and/or is being represented by legal counsel should be avoided. To engage in an investigation of such a subject is to invite an invasion of privacy suit. Such subjects are generally extremely wary, and so the most carefully prepared pretext can, and under such circumstances often does, prove unsuccessful.

2. A pretext that is very complex should be avoided. The greater the complexity, the greater the chance that the investigator will slip up as a result of becoming confused with his own story. Similarly, the use of more than one pretext name should be avoided. The investigator should select one name and use no other so that he becomes familiar with it and will react appropriately when addressed by it.

3. When conducting a pretext, the investigator must *never* use his real name or the name of the investigating company regardless of how simple the pretext appears to be.

4. Failure to anticipate logical questions and the appropriate response to them according to the pretext being used is a common problem. The investigator should use pretexts that he knows well so that he can reasonably anticipate logical questions and their appropriate answers. Failure to do so will result in a marked decline in his rate of success.

5. Failure to back off and discontinue efforts when it has become evident that the pretext is not going according to plan and there is little hope for recovery is a common problem. Such failure can result in the investigator's being exposed.

6. If the subject of the pretext should become aware that the investigator is not who he purports to be, the investigator should under no circumstances reveal the true identity of either himself or his client. For this reason it is desirable that the investigator park his car out of the area in which the pretext is being conducted. If the investigator has reason to suspect he is being followed, he should not return to his vehicle until he is certain that the tail has been lost or broken.

7. If it is ever necessary to sign something, the investigator must be sure to use the pretex name. It is easy for the investigator to mistakenly sign his real name if not consciously thinking about it, an act that would, without a doubt, be most embarrassing.

8. When conducting a pretext survey in a residential area, the investigator must make the survey appear authentic by interviewing some neighbors before and after the subject has been contacted.

PRETEXT EXAMPLES

While it is not possible to cover every consideration for the investigator engaged in pretext work, the following examples should serve to give the reader the understanding necessary to engage in this type of work and do a good job of it. The reader should understand that these examples are not intended to be hard and fast rules but are intended primarily to stimulate his imagination. Many times it is necessary to conduct the pretext in person; however, consideration should be given to the use of the telephone whenever possible. Should the telephone pretext be unsuccessful, it can be terminated much more easily and with less risk involved.

Inspection of Premises

This is a way to gain access to a residence to determine if such things as stolen merchandise are stored within. The investigator should know something about electrical installation, although no great knowledge is actually required. He should dress in work clothes, carry a clipboard and flashlight, and call when the subject himself is not home. The investigator could state that he represents a fire insurance underwriting firm that is insuring the premises in question. He can state that the insurance carrier wants a thorough inspection of the electrical wiring made before it renews the policy. Once permission to enter is granted, a thorough search of all areas should be made, including the basement, garage, attic, etc. While conducting the search, the investigator should examine the fuse box, electrical outlets, and switches, to make his search appear thorough and legitimate.

A variation of this pretext can be used when dealing with tract homes. The investigator states that there have been reports of the electrical wiring not being up to code and that he is checking homes to determine the status of their wiring. When conducting this type of pretext, it is desirable for the investigator to check other homes in the immediate area to lend an air of credibility to the pretext so that the subject does not become suspicious.

Disability Verification

A typical pretext that the investigator might use to obtain an interview with a claimant for the purpose of establishing the current status of his disability is as follows: The investigator should obtain several samples of food products and some preprinted questionnaire forms containing typical questions about the quality of the samples. The claimant is advised that the investigator represents a firm making a survey of the products for an advertising agency and that his cooperation and opinion would be helpful. In return for his cooperation he will receive a sample of the product. During the pretext interview the investigator can observe the subject in a relaxed manner in familiar surroundings. His alleged disability or lack of disability is more likely to be apparent under these circumstances.

Disability Verification, Female

The following is a pretext a female investigator might consider using to obtain an interview with a female claimant for the purpose of establishing the current status of her disability: The female investigator obtains a few cans of vegetables and removes the labels. She should have a preprinted food chart questionnaire prepared for the purpose of recording the results, to make the pretext appear official. The investigator approaches the claimant at her home and states that she represents a nationally known food packer (whose name is not known to her). The investigator explains that she is conducting a survey of housewives to determine for the client what type of packing is most preferred, such as in water, oil, etc. The claimant is asked to open the cans and prepare the vegetables on her stove and offer her opinion of each. To carry it even further, the investigator might suggest that the claimant invite a few friends from the neighborhood to participate.

Infringements

This pretext might be used to gain access to a plant for the purpose of determining if a violation of a patent, copyright, or trademark is being committed there. The investigator assigned should be able to appear as a student. He must, of course, be familiar with the suspected violation he is looking for, and he should carry a notebook. He can state that he is a journalism student assigned to write an article on that particular plant or industry and would like to gather some information for that project by observing their process, interviewing some employees, and possibly taking some pictures.

Warehouse or Garage

The following might be used to gain access to a warehouse, closed garage, or other area. The investigator dresses in casual clothes and purchases a leash suitable for walking a pet cat. The investigator then approaches the establishment in an agitated state, carrying the leash, and announces that he has been out walking his wife's Siamese cat, "Mitzi," and that it has gotten away from him. He states that he thinks the cat may have run inside the building in question and that he must find it before it gets lost or his wife will be furious. Naturally everyone is sympathetic and will probably even assist him in his search. Once inside, the investigator can make observations of whatever he is really seeking. He must, of course, continue the pretext by searching outside and down the street once he has completed his search of the building in question.

Whereabouts at a Specific Time

To establish the whereabouts of a person at a specific time and date, the following might be employed. The investigator obtains the license number of the subject's vehicle. He then approaches the subject and states that a vehicle with his license number was observed to be involved in a traffic accident on the date and time in question. The subject, of course, will deny the accusation, and the investigator can then ask him where he actually was. If the subject has no vehicle, the investigator could modify the pretext by stating that there was an injury in a supermarket and his name was furnished by a witness.

Once the subject's whereabouts have been determined, the investigator could conclude the pretext by saying the witness must have been in error and he (the investigator) will correct the matter.

Establishing Occupation

To establish a person's occupation and name of employer, the investigator might use the following pretext: He should obtain the subject's name, address, and general description. He should then approach the subject and state that he represents an automobile repossession agency and he is attempting to locate a "skip" with the same name as the subject's. Naturally, the subject will deny he is the same individual. The investigator should ask for the make and model of the subject's vehicle and the name of the subject's employer for purposes of verification, then apologize for any inconvenience caused to the subject and assure him that the records will be corrected.

An alternative pretext might be for the investigator to say that he is conducting a survey for a company that is contemplating the construction of a plant in the area and wishes to establish the availability of manpower locally. During the conversation the investigator can ask the subject (or his wife) to state where he is currently employed.

Locating Missing Persons

To locate a missing person, the investigator might use a pretext similar to the following: He should ascertain the person's last known address and contact one or more neighbors, stating that the subject left an article for storage with the investigator or that the investigator owes him some money and would like to return it.

Obtaining Handwriting Samples

To obtain a sample of someone's handwriting, the investigator could prepare a fact sheet on a fictitious accident that shows the subject as a witness, then bandage his writing hand so as to appear he would have great difficulty in writing. The investigator should state that he is investigating an accident and ask the subject for a statement. The subject will, of course, deny having seen the accident, whereupon the investigator should appear surprised and ask the subject to furnish a brief statement acknowledging that he was contacted by the investigator but has no knowledge of the accident.

Alternatively, with a supply of preprinted pretext forms containing questions concerning age, how long licensed to drive, make of car driven, number of miles driven each year, etc., the investigator approaches the subject and states he is conducting a survey for an automobile association. He requests that the subject complete the form.

PRETEXT TELEPHONE LINES

Because investigators must rely so heavily upon pretext investigation techniques, it is essential that they have available a number of props to assist them in their task of successfully executing a pretext, including pretext survey forms, pretext business letterheads, pretext identification cards, and a pretext telephone line.

The pretext line is a telephone line that the investigator has installed in his office that is not listed to his real name or business and is unpublished. The line is never to be used for the purpose of conducting normal business since that would only serve to jeopardize its effectiveness when using it for pretext work, which is the reason for securing the line in the first place.

The investigator will issue the pretext number when he is conducting pretext work over the telephone and it is necessary to give out a number so that the subject of the pretext may return the call for any number of reasons. It is also issued when the subject of a pretext desires to call the investigator's office of employment (the pretext business) to verify his employment. Because of the nature of pretext work, the people in the office who will have occasion to answer that telephone should be carefully and thoroughly instructed as to how that telephone should be answered. When a call is received over that line, the telephone should be answered by the last four digits of the phone number, not by announcing a business name. This is important, as the private investigator will use many different pretexts depending upon the needs of the particular case he is working on at that time. If the call is in response to an investigator posing as, for example, Mr. Richard Ames of Raymond and Associates, the party placing the call will most likely ask if he has not reached Raymond and Associates when he hears the telephone answered by the four digits only. He should, of course, be told that he has, in which case the caller will probably ask if Mr. Richard Ames is in or if he works there, depending upon the story that he has been given. The response should naturally be affirmative. If, when the telephone is answered announcing only the four digits, the caller asks whom he has reached, the person anwering the telephone should ask him whom he was calling.

In the event that someone should call the pretext line and ask for an investigator by his real name, the person answering the telephone should state that he does not know that person and also that he is not associated with that firm or company. One can safely assume at that point that something has gone wrong and the number is "hot," and the telephone company should be asked to issue a new number. Similarly, if someone should call on the real business line and ask for an investigator by his pretext name, he should be told that there is no one by that name there. A pretext number is good only so long as a pretext is successful. Should a person become suspicious after being given the number, it *is* possible for him to learn to whom the number has really been issued. Again, the number should be changed.

Chapter Eight

LOCATES
(WITNESSES AND MISSING PERSONS)

GENERAL CONSIDERATIONS

Nᴏᴛ infrequently an investigator will be called upon to establish the identities of witnesses to an event and their whereabouts. In other instances the investigator is called upon to establish the whereabouts of known persons who have for any number of reasons moved either without volunteering or perhaps even attempting to conceal their whereabouts. In the case of witnesses, the investigator can generally conclude that they are not attempting to cover their identity or whereabouts; they simply do not realize that they possess knowledge that is needed. When contacted, they will usually volunteer what they have observed. In cases where an important witness has moved, it will be necessary for the investigator to determine where he has moved.

In other instances, the investigator will be called upon to establish such things as the whereabouts of a missing heir, a person who owes a creditor money and has defaulted, or a missing spouse. The resourcefulness of the investigator will be challenged, and he must be thorough in his investigation if he is to succeed. If the investigator routinely plans his work well and is thorough, he will find that he can maintain an impressive percentage of success at this work.

LOCATING WITNESSES

When the investigator is charged with the task of establishing the identity of witnesses and their whereabouts, his course of action will depend largely upon the type of event they were witness to and the location. There will be a marked difference, for example, should the incident be an automobile accident as opposed to a mishap in a restaurant. If it is a mishap in a restaurant, the logical starting point would be to interview the employees to learn whether they observed the incident. When interviewing them, the investigator would make an effort to establish who else may have observed the event. The investigator would attempt to determine if there were other employees working at the time of the event and what others may have been patronizing the establishment at that time. Lists of reservations, if available, can often prove to be useful in this respect.

If, however, the event in question is an automobile accident, the investigator would logically start with the police report and the investigating officer, if the police were in fact summoned. The investigator should also consider the possibility of public transportation (bus, taxicab, etc.) passing by the scene at the time in question, or if there were people waiting for a bus at that time on that particular day, they should be interviewed. All people working and residing in the area should be contacted. When interviewing them, the investigator should attempt to learn exactly what useful information they may possess as well as attempt to develop other possibilities insofar as witnesses are concerned. He should determine at what time deliveries such as milk and mail are made and interview such people where appropriate.

The task of the investigator is to establish the identity of all persons who may have been in a position to observe the incident in question and then to interview them. When interviewing people in an effort to locate witnesses, he should conduct the interviewing at the same time and day of the week that the actual event took place. He will often be amazed at how much useful information can be developed in such instances, as a case can seemingly unravel in his hands.

LOCATING MISSING PERSONS

The following is a list of informational sources that often proves fruitful in the locating of missing persons:

1. All should be interviewed, using a pretext when necessary (refer to chapter on pretext investigations).
2. Subject's employer, if his place of employment is known
3. Subject's co-workers
4. Employment application — Such a record often reflects information such as names and addresses of personal references and next of kin, place and date of birth, and previous employment history and other miscellaneous information that may be helpful depending upon the circumstances.
5. Credit company — Inquiries are frequently exchanged between cities.

7. School records, if there is a school-aged member of the family
8. Records that are transferable such as church, lodge, professional organizations, etc.
9. Notice of change of address at the post office
10. Moving companies — They may possess useful information.
11. Telephone directory or directory assistance — This is a valuable source that is easily overlooked.
12. Mail receipts — To determine if the subject is in town, the investigator might send him a registered letter at his residence address to see if it is signed for.
13. Court records — These can prove to be helpful in certain instances.
14. Voter's registration
15. Driver's license and motor vehicle registration records

When attempting to locate a missing person, the investigator will at times find it necessary to contact persons using a suitable pretext. This is true in cases where a person's family or friends are aware of his whereabouts but are unwilling to divulge that information (refer also to the chapter on sources of information).

Family or relatives of a missing person may or may not have knowledge of the person's whereabouts. The parents of a male may or may not have heard from him since he left; however, a daughter is *much* more likely to make contact with her parents.

A single son is sometimes less distracted and more likely to contact home than a married son. One investigator has a saying that sums up his views on this topic: "A son is a son till he takes him a wife; a daughter's a daughter all the days of her life." An undistracted son is likely to contact home at some point; so, locating him through the parents or family may be possible. However, if he is married or has distractions such as a girl friend, he is less likely to contact home. However, the girl friend or wife is likely to contact home regardless of the status of her love life, and so locating her through family or parents may well be possible. Thus if the person to be located has a girl friend or wife with him, it may be more fruitful to attempt to determine his whereabouts by locating the girl friend or wife.

Chapter Nine

INDUSTRIAL AND COMMERCIAL
UNDERCOVER OPERATIONS

GENERAL CONSIDERATIONS

T HE annual dollar loss to business and industry because of dishonest employees cannot be estimated with complete accuracy, but it is known that the loss greatly exceeds that from major crimes such as burglary and robbery and thefts such as shoplifting. When comparing internal (employee) theft and external (nonemployee) theft, the incidence of internal theft tends to be significantly greater. In fact, it has been estimated by reliable sources that between 20 and 30 percent of all business failures are a direct result of employee theft (embezzlement), and one in ten bankruptcies result from the theft of information. The latter falls into the realm of business espionage, discussed in Chapter 12.

There is no question about the seriousness of internal crime, even though businesses tend to be more concerned about the less significant external crime problem. In the United States there is an annual loss of several billion dollars attributed to internal crime. With this in mind, it is apparent why these thefts have such a devastating effect upon business and industry. While it is true that in many instances an individual act of theft may be rather small and therefore appear to be insignificant, they accumulate rapidly. As an example, if five employees are stealing $5 each a day from a business, that amounts to $25 per day, $125 per week, and $6,250 per year. If the business is operating on a 7 percent net profit, it must generate yearly gross sales of $89,286 to break even on these seemingly insignificant $5 thefts.

It is because of internal theft that many commercial and industrial firms employ undercover operators. Because the problem comes from within, the most effective means of combating it is from within (along with utilizing sound business practices in all other areas). Although the firm employing such a service tends to think initially only of what it is doing to combat or curtail theft itself, it soon realizes a host of other benefits that result from an undercover (internal intelligence) operation.

104

An undercover investigator goes into a place of business and, while posing as an employee, becomes part of the landscape, so to speak, and slowly establishes rapport with the employees, placing an emphasis on those who are in a position that favors their engaging in activity that could be of interest to the client. It is essential that no one know the investigator's true purpose. This point cannot be over emphasized; because the fewer people in management who are aware of the operation, the better off everyone involved will be. Also, the client is generally not an investigator, and while his intentions may be honorable, if he is not properly counseled and controlled, he may inadvertently "blow the agent's cover." While the investigator is on the job, the client should never, under any circumstances, talk to him directly but direct any necessary communication to the agency by which the investigator is employed.

INTERNAL CRIME AND EMBEZZLEMENT

Internal theft, commonly referred to as *embezzlement*, is the taking of money or property that has, in one way or another, been entrusted to one's care or custody. The taking of *property* is the most common form of embezzlement.

There are few security and loss control experts who would not agree that businesses generally suffer greater theft losses as a result of internal theft than as a result of external theft, as already stated. There are several reasons for this; they include but are not limited to —

1. Employees have available to them not only the same opportunities to commit an offense as the outside thief but also additional opportunities. This includes access to many areas not normally accessible to nonemployees. Also, their hours of accessibility are generally greater. Hence, most merchandise is frequently and readily accessible to employees.
2. While the outside thief will generally commit an offense and then depart, the employee thief often establishes a system; the thefts are committed on an ongoing, and often escalating, basis. This systemized procedure, while it will vary in its degree of sophistication, may or may not involve other employees and/or nonemployees. Typically the embezzler works alone. However, organized internal theft rings do occur and can bankrupt a company very quickly.
3. Inadequate controls that permit small-scale internal theft are a laxness that also permits the problem to mushroom, and it usually will. Unlike external theft that is immediately evident to management, the internal problem, being thefts of stealth, often goes undetected until astronomical losses have been inflicted. Employee dishonesty losses are particularly serious and dangerous to a firm because it is difficult to make accurate advance estimates of the maximum possible or probable loss.

While the specific motives of the perpetrator will vary somewhat, there are four principal causes for employee theft (embezzlement):

1. Compulsive gambling
2. The desire to live beyond one's means
3. Alcoholism and other types of drug addition
4. Health problems of the employee or a family member, as affected by the astronomical increase in health care costs

Property that is particularly vulnerable is usually that with *high value and low volume/weight*. Embezzlement involving auto stores, for example, often involves the parts department.

The undercover investigator and the client being served should recognize two important elements that create a situation conducive to employee theft. They are the employer's lack of effective control over money and property and the belief by the employer that a long-term, trusted employee could not be an embezzler (thief). *Most* embezzlers are long-term, trusted employees. They are trusted and therefore less likely to be watched as closely, and they generally have greater access to money and/or property. Also, they have had time to devise a system for accomplishing the offense.

While management should not regard all employees as thieves or relate to them as such, controls should be established so that embezzlement will be revealed by *routine checks*. The undercover operation should not be regarded as the only ingredient necessary to prevent internal theft; rather, it should be used to test the system to determine how well the controls are working and whether it is necessary to modify the defenses.

THE NEED FOR SECRECY

In setting up and supervising an industrial and commercial operation, it is important that the investigator exercise all precautionary measures from the onset. Arrangements should be made to meet the client and discuss the forthcoming operation at a location other than the client's place of business. This will not only prevent employees from observing the meeting and becoming curious or suspicious but will also start the client thinking in terms of the secrecy that is so essential to the success of an operation of this nature. Arrangements should be made to send subsequent reports to the client's home or any other location that is mutually agreeable. Reports should never, however, be sent to the client's place of business, as the danger of their falling into the wrong hands is too great. There have been cases of an individual's private secretary, whom he believed he could trust, learning of an operation and alerting others.

The investigator should discuss the secrecy aspects of the operation with the client before commencing the operation. The client must be made to understand that he can tell no one about the operation, in part or its entirety, without first discussing such a move with the appropriate representative of the investigating agency. Further, already stated, he must never talk with the investigator while he is on the job. If a meeting with the client is necessary at any time *after* the operation has begun (and such a meeting is usually desirable) it also should be conducted at some location other than the client's plant where not likely to be observed. Further, experience has shown that it is desirable to have a middleman involved in an undercover operation so that it will not be necessary for the investigator to have direct contact with the client himself.

UNION ACTIVITIES

In conducting undercover operations, one area to be very careful of is reporting on union activities or collective bargaining processes of employees. There are federal laws against making such reports to management, and anyone intending to engage in undercover work would do well to obtain a copy of the federal statutes pertaining to such activities.

BILLING RATES

The billing rate for undercover operations will differ from that for other types of investigations. While an hourly fee is most common for general investigations, a daily fee for reports is more commonly the case with undercover operations. The rate for undercover operations is greatly reduced from what it would be were the client being charged the customary hourly rate for the time that the investigator spends working on the case. If the usual rate were charged, the investigator would not be competitive in price with other investigative agencies.

Also, because the undercover investigator will be working as an employee of the client, he should be paid by the client for the work he is doing within the client's business. Naturally, the investigator will be expected to put in a good day's work for the money he receives; if he does not, his foreman may terminate him. Therefore, the client is already paying a portion of the investigator's salary. Since this is true, the agency need not pay the investigator as much as normal to give him a very good total salary and likewise can afford to charge the client a reduced rate and still make a reasonable profit.

Also, a good undercover operation will often last for several months. If an agency were to employ a few good undercover investigators, it could have several operations going at one time and generate a considerable amount of revenue with a limited amount of time and effort. Taking all these factors into consideration, it is obvious why the billing rate for undercover work need not be as high per hour as for general investigations in order to make it a profitable area of endeavor.

CLIENT-INVESTIGATOR RESPONSIBILITY

Clients should be instructed that the undercover investigator is to be handled just like any other employee. He will be expected to perform his duties, whatever they may be, the same as anyone else working within the company. To begin with, the investigator should make application through the personnel department, which is the way any prospective employee acquires a job. The investigator should start his reporting with the initial job interview. In this way he will be reporting on all phases of the client's operation that he comes in contact with, and by so doing, he will make the client aware of conditions and procedures the way newcomers actually see them. After the hiring process, the investigator should write reports on how he is indoctrinated and trained into the company. This is important because the way he is handled is the way everyone is handled.

As stated earlier, the main reason many clients will authorize an undercover operation in the first place is because they feel, for any number of reasons, that one or more employees may be engaged in theft. The investigator assigned to the case must be familiar with the various ways a thief operating internally can steal from his employer. The investigator, to be of maximum benefit, must also be briefed as thoroughly as possible before he begins his investigation, so that he will be aware of the scope of the client's operation and who may be in positions that are most favorable to theft.

It is then the investigator's responsibility to effect penetration, or in other words, secure a job within the client's business, and slowly get to know and establish rapport with such employees. A word of caution is in order here, as the investigator can jeopardize the case should he attempt to gain the confidence of people too quickly. It is generally better for the investigator to place himself in a position whereby the subjects will draw him into their group rather than try to invite himself into their circle. It is also desirable in most cases that the investigator socialize with the subjects, not only on the job but off the job as well. If there is a favorite hangout, he should go there. Many times an investigator can secure more information over a beer at the local pub than he could in a month on the job.

The duties and responsibilities of an undercover investigator will be primarily the same, with minor variations, regardless of the type of establishment within which he is working. While working in a retail store, for example, he may be in a position to observe the activities of shoplifters. As an undercover investigator, his responsibilities in reporting and apprehending shoplifters are strictly those of any other employee in the store. If the other store employees are very aggressive in this respect, the investigator should assist to the extent that is expected of him. If, on the other hand, the store employees do not get involved but simply advise the store detectives, the investigator should do likewise. If there are store detectives, the investigator should include in his reports his observations concerning them.

ENTRAPMENT

One of the best methods by which to obtain information and evidence concerning employee theft is for the investigator to become involved with the employees who are engaged in such activity, but the investigator must exercise extreme caution and be fully aware of what constitutes entrapment. *The investigator must be careful never to suggest that a crime or irregularity be committed.* The investigator, may, however, go along with an idea once it has been suggested by someone else. In fact, he may even let it be known that he is open to suggestions or that he is seeking a means by which to make a little extra money, but he cannot actually suggest that an irregularity or crime be committed. It must be remembered that the purpose of the undercover operation is not to create more problems for the client but to solve existing ones. Entrapment is not something that pertains only to undercover operations; it applies to practically all phases of investigative work. Each investigator would do well to be fully familiar with exactly what constitutes entrapment. Legal advice is recommended.

REPORTS

Obviously, the investigator will not observe meaningful incidents such as employees actually engaged in theft every day; so, to give his reports a full and professional appearance, he should also report on anything else that could be of interest to management. It is not the investigator's responsibility to tell management how their plant or business should be run, but he should make them aware of how it is being run in their absence. Some additional things of interest to management would be the quality of supervision, employee morale, safety, fire hazards, shipping and receiving procedures and violations of same, drinking, gambling, use of drugs or narcotics on the job, sale of drugs or narcotics on the job, friction between employees or employees and supervisors, and the identities of both the troublemakers and the conscientious and loyal employees.

Most investigative companies that engage in a considerable amount of. undercover work have prepared checklists for their investigators' use. A checklist has value primarily in that an investigator can review it periodically to ensure that he is reporting on everything that he should be. Another good idea that helps to ensure professional-appearing reports is to make a report, positive or negative, concerning each area that has been covered.

For example, if the investigator has observed the time card procedures for a few days, and all is as it should be, he may make a comment to the effect that the time card procedure has been carefully observed for several days with no irregularities or abuses observed. While some may argue that such information would be of limited value to the client since there is no irregularity taking place in that particular area, the manager must not only know what is going wrong within his operation to correct it and thus run an efficient operation, he must also know what is going right. In other words, he must have a clear picture of his entire operation, not just a portion of it. If the investigator made no comment concerning the checking of time card procedures, management would have no way of knowing whether it had been looked into and what its status was.

Reporting methods such as this also serve to let the client know what the investigator is doing and what he is paying for. A report that states, "Nothing unusual occurred today," is not only nonprofessional in appearance; it is also vague. Such a report can mean that nothing in fact occurred, or it can indicate that the investigator is not doing the job expected of him. A client who is willing to pay for an undercover operation is genuinely concerned about where his money is going. Such a person will not pay long for a series of reports that simply state, "Nothing unusual occurred today."

The variety of things that can be reported on during an undercover investigation is endless. The investigator should attempt to place himself in the client's position and think in terms of what he would be interested in knowing about the operation were it his. The investigator should then put into report form anything that could in any way be of interest to the client. Some of the things he may view as being important may seem trivial to the client, while things that seem trivial to the investigator may be of paramount importance and interest to the client. The investigator, therefore, should attempt to be thorough in his reporting and let the client decide what may or may not be important. Again, it is not the responsibility of the undercover investigator to tell the client how to run his business but rather to make him aware of how it is being run in his absence. .

There are different schools of thought regarding reporting techniques for undercover operations. While some companies allow their undercover investigators to write reports in the first person, many companies require reports to be written in the third person for purposes of secrecy. When preparing a report in this manner, the investigator will include himself in it as if someone else wrote the report. A technique or method such as this has merit in that if someone unauthorized should happen to read the report he would not be able to identify the investigator. To teach an investigator to write reports in the third person takes time, but the one time a report does end up in the wrong hands makes the effort worthwhile. The investigator should remember also to send the reports to a location other than the client's place of business.

The investigator should use a number or other identifying trademark but never his real name. This should go without saying, especially if the reports are being written in the third person. It is also important that the investigator never refer to the company by name in his reports. The client's facilities should be referred to simply as "the company." All persons who have a need to will be aware of what "the company" is. No one else should possess this information.

When the reports go into the mail, there should be no return address upon the envelopes. These precautions are necessary as a safeguard against unauthorized persons reading the reports and identifying the investigator and the client facility. Someone from outside the company who does not recognize any of the subject's names will have no idea what company the reports pertain to. Should a report turn up missing in the mail, it will be a simple matter to have a copy from the investigator's file reproduced.

All these precautions and safeguards may appear, on the surface, to be a bit clandestine or cloak-and-dagger-ish, but they could save an investigator and his client a considerable amount of embarrassment, not to mention the operation itself, should a report be lost. Besides, once the investigator has gotten into the habit of operating in this fashion, it requires very little extra time, effort, or expense to add these small measures of security.

Chapter Ten

BODYGUARD SERVICE

GENERAL CONSIDERATIONS

IN many cases an investigator is called upon to safeguard an individual, or in other words, serve him as a bodyguard. The investigator when performing such a service should be in possession of certain specialized knowledge; there are certain basic fundamentals that should be observed to do the job effectively.

The most common reason an individual or firm will request this service is that someone will be, or is, frequently transporting large sums of money or other valuables such as jewelry. This service will also be requested when there have been threats made against someone's life or against members of the family.

When private investigative companies engage in this service, they generally conduct their operation in a manner simplified from that used by police departments or the Secret Service. The difference lies primarily in the size and sophistication of the operation, normally for reasons of cost. In all but exceptional cases, only one or two investigators will safeguard an individual. This contrasts sharply to the operations conducted by governmental agencies, who typically assign an entire team to provide security to an individual. Hence, there is a great difference between offering *bodyguard service* and an *executive protection program*.

Although cost typically results in one or two private investigators being assigned to safeguard an individual, such limited protection is not recommended. If an attacker dispatches a lone bodyguard, the subject is without protection; if there are two bodyguards, the subject is then left with only one. If the threat assessment suggests a potential terrorist attack, attempting to protect the subject with one or two lone guards would be no less than suicidal.

This chapter will offer a brief discussion of accepted methods and procedures for an executive protection program. Then, each investigator must assess each individual case and set up a protective program that finds the balance point between operational cost and effectiveness. For those desiring a more in-depth discussion of this topic, there is a book that deals specifically with it in considerable detail*.

RISK MANAGEMENT

Protecting against a criminal or terrorist attack, like anything else, requires planning. Failure to plan effectively will generally leave the investigator with a haphazard operation that is far less efficient than it could and should be. The results could well be fatal.

When setting up a protective program, the investigator should work within the basic *risk management framework* to ensure thoroughness and a high-quality operation. The framework is as follows:

1. *Hazard, problem, risk, or vulnerability identification and analysis* — This phase is critical since it is impossible to find solutions to a problem without first understanding what the problem consists of.
2. *Treatment techniques selection* — There is generally more than one potential solution to a problem. Once the problem and the various potential solutions have been identified, a choice that is consistent with needs, cost, and conveinience can be made.
3. *Implementation of the chosen techniques and methods* — Having identified the problems and decided how to treat them, the investigator must consider how, by whom, and by when the chosen techniques or methods will be implemented.
4. *Monitoring the results* — This is important to ensure that the chosen techniques are in fact appropriate, that they were properly implemented, and that they continue to be effective. Effectiveness can diminish if the program becomes lax or if circumstances that initially justified the chosen measures change. Should effectiveness diminish, it may be necesssary to repeat steps 1 through 3.

VULNERABILITY

During the planning stages many things must be considered, such as who the potential attackers are, their capabilities, and the various points and locations of vulnerability that must be dealt with. As a general rule, terrorist attacks are planned well in advance. The point of attack is very often one of the following:

---

*Siljander, Raymond P.: *Terrorist Attacks, A Protective Service Guide for Executives, Bodyguards, and Policemen.* Springfield, Charles C Thomas Publisher, 1980.

1. As the victim is either arriving or leaving a building
2. As the victim is entering or alighting from a motor vehicle
3. While the victim is driving or riding in a car, when its movement can be interrupted
4. When the victim is attending a speaking engagement

Many types of weapons have been employed to date. The following is a list of weapon types used, in the order of their frequency of use:

1. Handguns
2. Explosives
3. Rifles
4. Blades and impact weapons
5. Shotguns
6. Machine guns
7. Poison

As would be expected, not all attacks result in a fatality. Some weapon types have proven to be more effective than others, thus resulting in a higher percentage of deaths. The following list gives weapons in the order of their past success as lethal assassination instruments:

1. Poison
2. Machine guns
3. Rifles
4. Blades and impact weapons
5. Shotguns
6. Handguns
7. Explosives

CORPORATE-LEVEL DEFENSES

A firm fearing the potential of a coordinated criminal or terrorist type of attack should —

1. *Maintain a low profile,* at least as much as conditions will permit,
2. *Gather pertinent intelligence data* — A continued source of data is essential to stay abreast of the problem; the sources of information will depend upon the nature of the problem — and
3. *Maintain physical security* — Physical security is essential at the place of residence of those affected, at the place of business, and, although more difficult to accomplish, during transit.

PLANNING AN ATTACK

While the problem is analyzed and solutions are chosen, the investigator must understand the method that is used by a terrorist group to plan an attack, whether in the form of an abduction or an assassination. Unless he understands the basics involved, he cannot properly defend against it. The degree of sophistication in the planning of the attack will depend upon the resources of the individual or group in question. The basic procedure will remain the same, however.

The planning of an attack will generally consist of three phases. This holds true whether the attackers are a political terrorist group or a reasonably well coordinated group of criminals. The three phases are —

1. Study of the intended victim,
2. Vulnerability analysis, and
3. Development of an operational plan.

Study of the intended victim includes gathering pertinent data on the individual from any source and also a physical surveillance of the intended victim. *Vulnerability analysis* can be undertaken only after the first phase has been completed. During this second phase, surveillance of the intended victim will continue so as to remain abreast of his/her daily activities. The vulnerability analysis utilizes the information obtained during the first phase to determine at what times and places the intended victim will be most vulnerable. *Development of an operational plan* is done after the second phase has been completed, when it has been determined what time and location will afford the greatest likelihood of a successful attack and subsequent escape. Developing an operational plan is simply determining how to actually make the attack.

ADVANCE SURVEYS

When the subject will be travelling out of town, it is important that an investigator procede him/her and make proper advance preparations for such things as transportation and lodging. The extent of the advance work will depend upon circumstances, of course.

During the advance survey the investigator must consider protection needs during movement and at fixed locations. All routes should be traveled to identify any points where difficulties could be encountered, and safe havens should be established along with potential alternate routes. Safe havens can be police stations, fire stations, hospitals, and military bases. During the advance survey, a simple floor plan of any motels to be patronized should be obtained.

During the advance survey, it is desirable to have a person with appropriate knowledge/experience conduct a *countersniper survey* in areas such as motels. The individual should attempt to identify all potential sniper vantage points within a range of 500 to 600 yards.

BODYGUARDS

The bodyguard is a very essential element of the total protective program. Unfortunately, the bodyguard is the most often misused element of a protective effort. In too many instances, when the need for protection is recognized, the need for a well-analyzed team effort is not recognized, and the desired level of protection is attempted using only one or two bodyguards. In other instances where a high level of threat exists and emphasis is placed on a well-planned protection program but no attack takes place within a resonably short period of time, the level of protection is, for purposes of cost and convenience, greatly reduced.

The bodyguard represents the innermost protective zone; it is the investigator in that position who must engage any attacker who manages to circumvent the outer security zones and must usher the victim to safety.

The task of a bodyguard is a challenging one, as is the total protective effort at all levels. The very nature of the job is challenging because an effort must be made to accompany the person being protected and provide protection while maintaining as low a profile as possible and causing a minimum degree of interruption in the life-style of the person being protected. This task if often complicated by varying degrees of uncooperativeness on the part of the person being protected. It would behoove anyone needing protection to cooperate fully with the protective force. It is poor judgment to retain protective services and then fail to abide by the recommendations made.

If dealing with a highly uncooperative client, and the threat level is at all great, the investigator would do well to discontinue the case, since his ability to protect a person adequately involves successfully avoiding the attack. An uncooperative client will make it difficult to avoid the attack, and often it is the bodyguards who are killed. If the client will not cooperate to a *reasonable* extent, it would be wise to withdraw from the case.

When two or more investigators are assigned to protect an individual, circumstances will often suggest to them the best placement of themselves and the person being protected. figure 10-1 offers some ideas.

GENERAL CONSIDERATIONS FOR BODYGUARDS

1. The bodyguard should always remain alert, anticipate possible threats, and have some type of plan in mind as to how a threat will be handled.

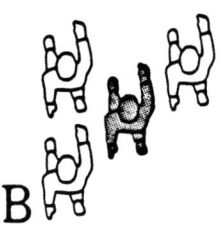

Figure 10-1. Bodyguard positioning while walking: A — wedge formation, B — modified wedge formation, C — box formation, D — box-wedge formation

2. He should watch the hands of anyone in close proximity, as it is the hands that will wield the weapon.
3. If an attack occurs, he should *attack the weapon, not the person.* The objective is to immobilize the weapon.
4. He should not look directly at suspicious persons. He should avoid alerting them to the fact that they are suspect and possibly causing them to launch the attack prematurely and/or from a distance that precludes proper intervention and neutralization of the weapon.
5. It is better to avoid an attack then to attempt to neutralize it once it occurs; so the bodyguard and person he is protecting should retreat if a threatening situation appears to be developing.
6. If an attack occurs, one bodyguard should intercept the attacker(s) while other escorts the victim to safety.
7. When under attack, it is better to retreat than proceed, since additional attackers may be spotted along the intended route.
8. The bodyguard must be aware that diversions are sometimes used to distract and confuse.

9. When walking, the bodyguards should provide the subject with a protective envelope by properly positioning themselves in relation to him/her.
10. When an attack occurs and the weapon cannot be attacked, one tactic is to throw anything that will tend to obstruct the attackers' vision.
11. When entering a room or hallway, the person being protected should be preceded by an investigator/bodyguard, who will ascertain that the area is safe.

The weapons to be used will not be discussed here since they depend greatly upon the training and skill of the investigators involved and upon the laws within a particular area of operation.

Body armor, sometimes refered to as a bullet-proof vest, has merit and should be given consideration. If used under conditions that justify them, these vests could well save a life. There are many types available; the investigator should contact the various manufacturers for promotional materials.

Communications are important; everyone involved must be kept in contact with each other and with a base unit if there is one. Communication needs must be established according to the particular operation. Usually, however, portable radios will be essential; they are available from a number of different manufacturers with various features. One useful feature is a remote microphone, as illustrated in Figure 10-2.

DRIVING TECHNIQUES

During periods of transit, effective protection becomes difficult, and it is during these periods that many abduction and assassination attempts occur. For this reason, the person driving the vehicle transporting the potential victim should have special training in high-performance driving and in the various techniques and methods for eluding an attacker, overrunning roadblocks, and using the vehicle as a weapon. Although the reader will be made aware of some of the things that can be done with the automobile, it is beyond the scope of this chapter to discuss in detail the manner in which the various techniques are actually executed. The book *Terrorist Attacks* goes into considerable detail however, and there are specialized schools that train drivers in such techniques. Such training is desirable because nothing can replace behind-the-wheel instruction from a qualified instructor.

High-speed driving is something that most drivers are not qualified to do without proper training. Such driving is truly a multiple task performance that allows for little error on the part of a driver and his vehicle. The kinetic energy of a vehicle in motion is tremendous, and it quadruples each time the speed of

Figure 10-2. Bodyguards and other protective personnel can wear the radio over or under the clothing using an earphone and external microphone. (Courtesy of Motorola)

the vehicle doubles; the faster the car goes, the greater the danger. In addition, as speed and levels of energy increase, the coefficient of friction between the road surface and the tires decreases. Also, braking efficiency is greatly reduced. High-performance driving schools discuss these factors in detail and also offer instruction on ways to control *weight transfer* of the vehicle and *spring loading,* both of which can be critical during high-speed driving. Also taught is the proper path to take when traveling through curves and making turns.

An attack upon a vehicle from another vehicle, using firearms, is generally accomplished with the attacking vehicle overtaking and passing the victim's vehicle. The gunmen, generally two on the passenger's side, begin firing when in the victim's blind spot and continue firing until their vehicle is far enough ahead of the victim's that too great an angle exists to continue firing. The time duration of such an attack is typically 10 to 15 seconds. The best counter generally is to brake hard, making a panic stop, to shorten the duration of the attack and to disrupt the aim of the gunmen.

When necessary, curbs can be driven over at speeds up to, and in some instances exceeding, thirty miles per hour. The important consideration is to strike the curb at an angle of 30 to 45 degrees. Such an angle will prevent losing control or damaging the vehicle or its tires.

At times it is necessary for a driver to reverse direction. This can be done by making a conventional turnaround, or it can be done using either a *forward 180-degree turn* or a *reverse 180-degree turn.* Both are precision maneuvers that allow one to make a complete turnaround while using very little road width. Also, the time necessary to execute such a maneuver is measured in seconds. Figure 10-3 depicts a forward 180-degree turn. Such a maneuver can be used to elude a pursuer or to retreat from a roadblock.

When a roadblock is encountered, the best course of action is usually to retreat. If that is not possible, it is usually necessary to overrun the roadblock. To simply drive around the roadblock can leave one victim to a concentrated volley of gunfire. Hence, it is important to attempt to neutralize as many attackers as possible, or those with the most threatening weapons. Figure 10-4 illustrates a vehicle overrunning a roadblock and the effect it has upon an attacker who foolishly took cover behind the vehicle. Generally a stationary vehicle roadblock should be struck at a speed not to exceed fifteen to twenty miles per hour, and it is important to keep the accelerator fully depressed while ramming through and depressed after the breakthrough has been made. Failure to do so can result in the engine stalling. If a pursuit occurs after the breakthrough, running will probably be futile, since the vehicle's cooling system is usually damaged. Accordingly, if a pursuit results, the investigator would do well to consider becoming the aggressor and turning upon the attacker, using the vehicle in as violent a manner as possible. If the investigator does not prevail almost immediately, however, he will probably lose.

Figure 10-3. (A) Victim, approaching a stationary vehicle roadblock, has placed the car in neutral gear and adjusted speed to about forty miles per hour. (B) Driver has snapped the steering wheel to the left and applied the emergency brake to cause the rear wheels to stop rotating (special equipment is also available for this). (C) Driver releases the emergency brake, goes quickly into low gear, and applies full engine power. (D) Vehicle has rotated a full 180 degrees, and driver then accelerates out of the kill zone. Three seconds were required to accomplish the turnaround. (Photos by Ken Siljander)

Figure 10-4. (top) Driver approaching the roadblock stops about thirty to fifty feet from it. (bottom) After stopping, the driver accelerates hard towards the roadblock, vehicle striking the rear fender or wheel area and driving the vehicle into the attacker. Driver keeps full engine power applied during and after the impact; he leaves the scene, breaking *visual* contact, as soon as possible. (Photos by Chris Reed and Ken Siljander)

Just as there are a number of methods for overrunning a roadblock, there are also a number of methods of using a vehicle to eliminate another vehicle, often one much larger and heavier. The knowledge of such techniques is useful to the investigator whether he is driving the vehicle being attacked or driving an escort vehicle. Again, discussing such techniques in detail is beyond the scope of this chapter, but basically they involve using total vehicle weight to apply eccentric forces upon the other vehicle. Once spinning more than 28 degrees off its axis, a vehicle cannot be recovered by counter steering.

Figure 10-5 illustrates a vehicle using its total weight, evenly distributed, to force a much heavier vehicle off the road by applying the force to only that weight resting on the front wheels. This method is effective if done quickly. Figure 10-6 illustrates how applying force to the rear quarter-panel of a vehicle will cause it to spin out of control.

Figure 10-5. One of many *vehicle elimination* techniques: Oldsmobile (3,700 lbs.) forces a Lincoln Continental (5,500 lbs.) off the road. (Photo by Chris Reed)

If a vehicle is to be used for escort purposes, various modifications are worth consideration, such as a reinforced frame and bumpers, smoke screen equipment, gun ports, a high-intensity light for extended visibility or attacker disruption, armoring to provide bullet resistance, sirens and tear gas equipment.

BOMB THREATS

When it is suspected that a bombing threat may be present, all areas that could contain an explosive device should be searched. In the event that anything suspicious is found, it should be left untouched. The area should be vacated, and the authorities contacted. Incoming mail should also be regarded with care to avoid problems with a letter/package bomb. Common warning signs to be alert for include:

1. Foreign return address
2. Address done by hand
3. Address to a specific person, sometimes marked "personal"
4. Air mail
5. Extra postage due to weight
6. Greater weight than a normal letter, also greater thickness
7. Stiffness
8. Oil stains
9. Some metal content such as wires

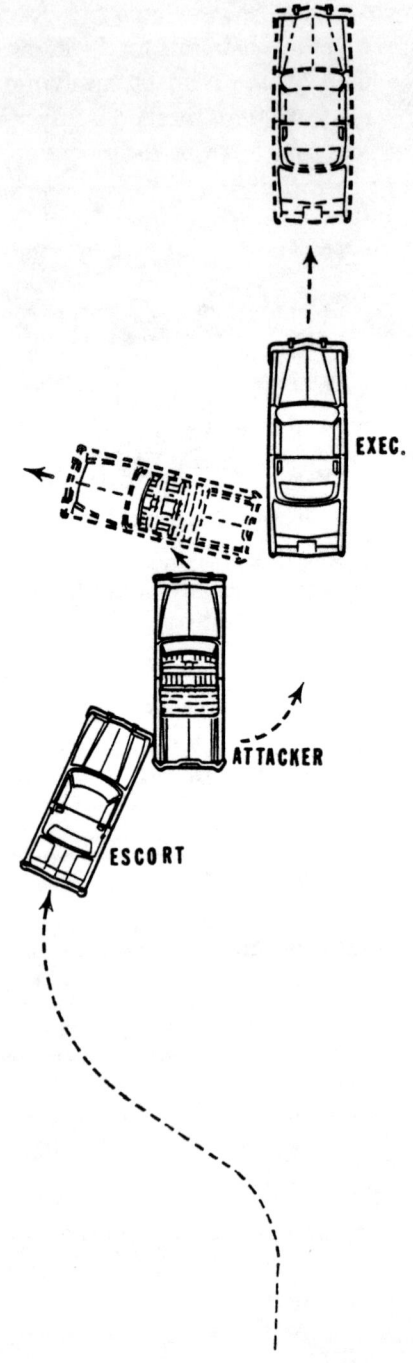

Figure 10-6. An escort vehicle can dispatch (eliminate) an aggressor vehicle by using his own vehicle to apply eccentric forces to the other vehicle. There are many variations of this basic technique.

SNIPERS

An advance team should consider the sniper threat at locations that will be visited and attempt to locate any potential sniper vantage points. Any sniper equipped with a high-powered rifle and telescopic sight presents a very real danger indeed.

Because it is possible to obtain telescopic sights for rifles that have a light-gathering capability similar to that of binoculars, there are exceptionally few areas in an urban setting where a properly scoped rifle cannot effectively be used at night at considerable distances, often 200 to 300 yards or more. Hence, distance and nighttime potential make the sniper a serious threat. Figure 10-7 illustrates a photographed observation through a twelve-power telescopic sight of a subject 100 yards away. The kill probability would be extremely high.

Figure 10-7. Photographed observation through a twelve-power telescopic rifle sight of a victim 100 yards away; the kill probability under such circumstances would be very high.

Chapter Eleven

AUTOMOBILE ACCIDENT INVESTIGATION AND RECONSTRUCTION

INVESTIGATION

Ａ N investigator will generally become involved in a motor vehicle accident investigation several days, sometimes several months, after the accident occurred. He will generally be working for either an insurance company or an attorney. If working for an attorney, he may be investigating on behalf of either the plaintiff or the defendant. It is important to note that regardless of which side the investigator may find himself representing, he should at all times strive to obtain facts and present them without any attempt to slant his findings in favor of his client. Any attempt to misrepresent the facts will not help his client but can only have an adverse effect. Slanting the facts would also lower the investigator's standing within his profession.

Investigating an accident scene is not something any investigator should attempt without proper preparation. There are several good publications available that treat this subject in depth, and in any major city there are some good investigators that specialize in this field. An investigator that tends to pursue this specialty must acquire a basic knowledge of the field and should then work closely with an experienced accident investigator for a sufficient time before striking off on his own. This, of course, is true of any specialty areas in which the investigator intends to engage . There are courses taught by colleges and universities that can greatly assist the fledgling accident investigator, and some accredited schools even specialize in this field. Many present-day accident investigators and accident reconstructionists obtained their early training and experience through military or law enforcement agencies.

In conducting the actual investigation, the investigator should first obtain a copy of the police report, statements, and any photographs that may have been taken at the scene. If no photographs were taken at the scene, the investigator should attempt to secure photos of the vehicles himself if the vehicles are still available and have not been repaired. When photographing a damaged vehicle, the investigator should take four direct views of each side, front, and rear. A view of the license plate should be included for identification purposes. Close-up shots should be taken of any and all small points of importance. When taking close-up photographs, it is important to include a scale for size reference, as well as an overview so that it is obvious on what vehicle and where on that vehicle the point of interest exists.

Photographs should be taken of anything that may have any possible significance. If a photograph later appears to have no bearing it can always be disregarded, but once the vehicles are repaired, the photos of the damage may be the only thing the accident reconstructionist, should his services be required, has to work with. So, the investigator should not economize on photographs.

When taking photographs of damaged vehicles, the investigator should be sure to conduct a close physical examination of the damaged vehicles' mechanical condition as well..Such an examination should include the braking system, headlamps, tail lamps, and turn signals, as well as the condition of tires and wiper blades if it was raining at the time the accident occurred.

The next step should be to attempt an interview with the investigating officer. The interview, if possible, should be conducted at the scene of the accident, and the police officer should be asked to bring any personal notes or any additional information he may have regarding the case. The extent of what can be obtained from the investigating officer will depend largely upon him and his departmental policy. Obviously, it would be in the investigator's best interest to conduct himself in a polite and unassuming manner because the police officer is under no obligation to cooperate with him.

The investigator, when interviewing the police officer at the scene, can ask him to point out such things as the following:

1. Point of impact
2. Direction of travel of the vehicles prior to impact
3. Any obstructions that may have been a contributing factor
4. Position of witnesses, if any

The officer should be asked to give a description of the damage done to each vehicle as well as his estimate of the speed at which each vehicle was traveling.

Some additional things on which the officer should be queried include the following:

1. Whether either party made any statements or admissions of guilt
2. His opinion regarding the condition of each driver
3. Any arrest made at the scene, specifying who was charged, the nature of the charges, and the disposition of the case (the officer may not be aware of the disposition, in which case, the investigator must obtain that information himself.)
4. The officer's opinion of who was at fault

5. Any other information the investigator deems appropriate, depending upon the specific circumstances

If no photographs were taken at the scene, the investigator should photograph the scene with views of the approaches upon which each driver was traveling as well as any contributing factors such as view obstructions. The investigator should also make a diagram of the accident scene and include measurements of all pertinent items.

If there has not been a great time lapse, it may be desirable to take color photographs of any personal injuries that resulted from the mishap.

The next step of the investigation should be an interview of the principals and witnesses. The investigator should carefully consider the interests of all who are interviewed and talk first with those who have no vested interest in the outcome of the case. He should take advantage of the element of surprise when conducting the interviews by not telephoning ahead for an appointment. This reduces the possibility of receiving a fabricated statement. Questioning of the witnesses should be very thorough and include all observations made prior to, during, and after the event. Any comments overheard by the witnesses should also be included, along with their opinion as to who may have been at fault.

When interviewing principals and witnesses, the investigator should not talk with the other party if he is being represented by legal counsel. It would be highly unethical to do so and could result in a lawsuit for invasion of privacy.

Whenever weather and road conditions appear to have been a factor, the investigator should obtain a copy of the U.S. Weather Bureau report for the weather conditions in effect at the time of the accident.

ACCIDENT RECONSTRUCTION

Should an accident result in very great property damage or injuries and/or death, it may be necessary, after a thorough investigation of the accident, to employ the services of an accident reconstuctionist. The average accident investigator does not possess the training and experience necessary to engage in this activity, and should he attempt to do so, he will only discredit himself and jeopardize the client's case. The services of an accident reconstructionist are rather expensive and therefore should be used only in the more difficult and severe cases.

The accident reconstructionist is a highly skilled specialist. It takes many years of training and practical experience to acquire the knowledge necessary to be recognized as an expert in this field. Should the accident investigator choose to pursue this field, he will find that although it is not an easy area of endeavor, it can be both challenging and rewarding.

Chapter Twelve

BUSINESS AND INDUSTRIAL ESPIONAGE

GENERAL CONSIDERATIONS

MANY businesses have a great deal to lose should a competitor gain possession of information pertaining to such things as formulas, processes, clientele, production capacity, future plans for expansion, market research, bids for contracts, and research and development. Industrial/business espionage is conducted by one U.S. firm against another and by foreign firms and foreign governments against U.S. firms.

The best way for a firm to assess its security and possible investigative needs in this area is to determine what it has that could benefit a competitor and what it could lose were a competitor to gain possession of such information. If a firm determines that it in fact has something to lose, and also determines specifically what it has to lose, it is then in a position to identify ways in which losses could occur and methods by which such loss potentials can best be treated. When concerning itself with the problem of counter-espionage, the firm should work within the basic risk management framework (*see* Chapter 10).

PERSONNEL HAZARDS

Without a doubt, the greatest hazard to a company's sensitive information is its employees. Employees present a risk to proprietary information primarily through such things as loose talk resulting from company pride in processes or products or thoughtlessness in talking about information without being aware of its confidential nature. There is also the danger of information being discussed where it can be overheard by unauthorized persons. Employees may also disclose information as a result of bribes, blackmail, or a desire for revenge for such things as having been passed over on a promotion, being underpaid, or having a generally unsatisfactory relationship with management.

In some instances the employee may have secured a job with a particular company for the sole purpose of obtaining information.

PERSONNEL SECURITY MEASURES

There are many possible security measures that may be considered for safeguarding against personnel hazards, and usually the security program will involve not one but a combination of several considerations. Initially, the company should consider and develop a *need to know* policy and enforce it. If there are employees who have no need to know about certain information, they should not be permitted to possess it. In some cases it is necessary for an employee to possess part of the information regarding a certain program but not all of it. When this is the case, he should possess only that information essential to the performance of his job. Every individual who possesses or has access to sensitive information that he does not need compounds the threat of a security leak. When it is necessary for certain individuals to possess secret information, they should be made aware of its sensitive nature and instructed on how it must be treated.

Companies who stand to lose a great deal, should they have an employee misusing sensitive information, cannot afford to hire and promote personnel without carefully scrutinizing their life-styles and backgrounds. Pre- and post-employment investigations will often serve to disclose associations with undesirable organizations. Also, if a prospective employee or an employee being considered for promotion to a sensitive position is living a life-style that exceeds his means, he will be vulnerable to bribes. Similarly, if an individual is a problem drinker or prone to other indiscretions, he will tend to be more vulnerable to extortion. It is for such reasons that pre- and postpromotional investigations are important. The cost of such investigations is inconsequential when compared to what a company may stand to lose should its proprietary information be misused. Further, even something as simple as an executive's travel plans should be considered proprietary; it takes little imagination to know how sensitive such information would be in the hands of someone desiring to abduct or assassinate the individual, for example.

SECURITY OF CONFIDENTIAL DOCUMENTS

Not totally unrelated to the hazards presented by persons to confidential information is the physical security of documents containing such information. The need to know policy was discussed earlier, and proper security of documents is an essential part of it; a company cannot implement and enforce such a policy and expect it to be successful if the sensitive material is available for all to read. Consequently, provisions must be made for the safeguarding of all documents and printed matter reflecting confidential information. When such documents are not actually in use, they should be locked in quality filing cabinets with high-quality locking devices. It is also desirable that confidential documents be appropriately marked so that they can be readily identified as such. This will help to ensure that they are treated and handled according to policy.

Assuming that the documents have been marked according to policy and also that they are contained in quality cabinets, it is then important that the filing cabinets be located in an area that affords the degree of physical security consistent with the particular needs. If the information is of an extremely sensitive nature, it may be desirable to post a guard to control entry to the area. A proper and strict identification policy is recommended for such areas. When there are visitors, they should be required to sign in and out and also to wear an appropriate visitor identification tag. It may be necessary in some cases to have a trained guard escort guests and service personnel to and from the area.

DISPOSAL OF PROPRIETARY WASTE

The manner in which confidential documents are handled is very important, but of equal importance is the way such documents are disposed of after their usefulness has expired, if the information remains sensitive. It is a well-known fact that rummaging through trash is a good source of intelligence data, and anyone seeking a company's proprietary information will certainly not overlook this method.

The best method for disposal of waste material will depend upon various circumstances, but one of the best methods to date is to feed the documents into a shredding machine. If the papers are destroyed by burning, it is important that the fire be attended until all papers are totally consumed.

Finally, the persons responsible for destroying confidential documents must be trustworthy, for they are in a unique position to effectuate a compromise.

COMPUTER SECURITY

It is not the purpose of this book to offer an in-depth discussion of physical security, nor would it be appropriate to offer more than an overview of the specialized topic of computer security, but the investigator should understand some of the basic concepts.

While computer equipment (electronic data processing, or EDP) offers a great deal to the business world, it also presents a new area of vulnerability.

Without appropriate EDP security measures, a firm with something significant to lose will be vulnerable. The investigator becoming involved in an investigation in some way concerned with the theft of information will be more comfortable if he understands that there is nothing mysterious or exotic about EDP security.

First, security of the computer facility against vandalism, sabotage, and espionage is important. Typical security measures are appropriate, such as locks, alarms, and access control of employees and nonemployees. Second, when possible, employees working in the computer area should have tasks divided and assigned in such a way that no one person is responsible for all phases of a job. This will decrease their ability to effectuate a compromise. It is helpful to note that computer fraud or embezzlement is most often committed by employees, while espionage is committed by nonemployees, but either group can commit either offense.

While effective computer security is costly and can be very complex, it basically boils down to accomplishing *physical control of data* and *work division*. Monitoring the effectiveness of the security program is an important ingredient. Effective security controls reduce the chance for problems, usually facilitate quicker detection of a compromise, and make the investigator's task when dealing with a computer security problem easier.

DEFENSIVE METHODS AGAINST ELECTRONIC EAVESDROPPING

General Considerations

While the scope of this book does not permit an in-depth and detailed discussion of the interception of wire and oral communications, also known as *electronic eavesdropping* or *audio surveillance*, and the defense methods against such practices, a brief discussion of the basic conventional methods of electronic surveillance and appropriate countermeasures will be useful.

Although there are many obstacles that make the job of the electronic eavesdropper a challenging task, the basic concept of *conventional* techniques is not difficult. In fact, almost anyone with a basic understanding of electricity and communications systems will find that he has the necessary background for such practices, at least on an elementary level.

There are federal laws regulating and limiting such activities as bugging a room or tapping a telephone line. The federal laws were needed, and the penalty is severe if someone is found in violation. When convicted, that someone may be not only penalized by the criminal court but civilly liable for damages arising from his illegal activities. So, this discussion is meant only to aid the investigator in understanding the threat of audio surveillance so that he is better able to defend against it. The reader should also be cautioned about the risk of electrocution when engaging in debugging activities; extreme care must be exercised when examining unknown wires.

There are basically three methods that may be employed to intercept wire or oral communications:

1. Tapping the telephone line
2. Concealing a microphone and its wires on the premises
3. Concealing a radio transmitter on the premises

A wide range of equipment may be employed, depending upon the eaves-dropper's degree of sophistication and the money he has with which to operate, but the basic essentials necessary for eavesdropping can often be purchased over the counter by anyone for a modest cost. On the other hand, much of the equipment that is manufactured specifically for eavesdropping is very expensive, highly sophisticated, and not available to the average person. Such equipment and the promotional literature for it are often available only to bona fide law enforcement agencies upon written request on their official letterhead.

The more conventional eavesdropping equipment includes automatic voice starters that will activate a tape recorder when a predetermined level of sound is present and then automatically stop the recorder when the sound ceases. Telephone line recorders do the same job as an automatic voice starter, except they activate a tape recorder in a telephone tap. Telephone number decoders will print the time, date, and number dialed each time the telephone in question is used; equipment is available for dial or push-button phones. Finally, there is an array of miscellaneous items, such as miniature microphones and radio transmitters built into cigarette lighters and pens. Telephone lineman's test sets are also useful to the eavesdropper.

Wiretaps

Monitoring conversations being conducted over the telephone system is not difficult; it can be accomplished using an induction coil, which does not require that an actual physical connection to the line be made. To make a physical tap is not difficult. however, and the equipment needed is minimal. This is not to imply, though, that some eavesdroppers do not use some very expensive and highly sophisticated equipment.

Generally, the eavesdropper will attempt to tap a telephone line at a time when the phone is not in use by the subscriber. This is done as a precaution against the subscriber's hearing the distinctive click that could make him suspicious.

When seeking out a telephone tap, the investigator is looking for anything that is foreign to the telephone system. Whether the telephone line has been tapped by means of an induction coil, by means of a capacitance-coupling, which is simply the wrapping of leads around the telephone lines to pick up the effects of the magnetic field that builds up around a wire carrying an electrical current, or by means of a physical connection, there are only certain points at which the tap may effectively be accomplished. Some of the locations are more readily accessible than others, and the person charged with the task of locating the tap must be very thorough in his physical search if detection is to be ensured.

The eavesdropper, if he has access to the building housing the phone, may install his equipment at any point between the telephone and the terminal box on the side of the building. If the tapper does not have access to the building, he may attach his apparatus to the terminal box on the outside of the building, or where the line connects to the telephone pole. (If the telephone to be tapped is in an apartment building, the eavesdropper's task is simplified, because the terminal box is usually in a utility room that is easily accessible.) Or, he may tap at the junction box, where the subscriber's wires join a cable route. To tap at the junction box, however, requires the tapper to have a very good understanding of what he is doing, and only an experienced and well-trained eavesdropper will normally attempt such a connection. The practitioner with less experience will generally choose to install the tap at some point between the telephone itself and the telephone pole.

While a subscriber's telephone can be monitored in the central office of the telephone company, checking that location is beyond the scope of the investigator's responsibility. The appropriate official within the telephone company should be contacted if such a tap is for some reason suspected. Such a tap is unlikely, however.

This nontechnical discussion of how a telephone line is tapped should make the reader realize that there is nothing magical or mysterious about wiretapping. The basic principles are indeed simple; however, some of the equipment employed and its implementation can be sophisticated.

Hidden Microphones and Radio Transmitters

In a conventional telephone tap, only those conversations actually being conducted over the telephone may be monitored. In many cases that will not produce the desired results, and the eavesdropper may decide to conceal one or more microphones or radio transmitters. The eavesdropper will in some cases make a minor alteration to the wiring within a telephone so that its microphone will become active and pick up all sounds within a reasonable distance from the unit. The eavesdropper can then tap the telephone line in the usual manner and monitor conversations taking place near or over the telephone. Detection of that type of alteration is not difficult and will be discussed later in this section.

The eavesdropper planting a microphone or radio transmitter is faced with some very definite problems, and it is to the investigator's advantage to recognize what those problems are, since locating such devices will be easier as a result. Bugging a room using a microphone can present obvious problems in all but unique situations because of the necessity of concealing the wire that must travel between the microphone and the recording or transmitting apparatus, for example. It is for this reason that radio transmitters are often preferred by eavesdroppers.

There is a wide range of size and quality among transmitters. However, in spite of the small size of many eavesdropping devices, placing them where they will not only avoid detection but will be most efficient in picking up and transmitting the desired sounds is not always an easy task. If the bug is placed on the floor, under a piece of furniture such as a sofa or easy chair, the sound of people walking about and of the furniture being moved will have a tendency to obliterate any conversations that may occur within the area. Air conditioners, fans, radios, and television sets also interfere with the efficiency of a bug.

When called upon to search a room or building for electronic eavesdropping devices, the investigator will naturally be concerned with telephone taps, hidden microphones, and radio transmitters. While there are many electronic aids for debugging, *the most important phase of any debugging operation is the physical search.*

Early in the search the investigator should endeavor to learn who previously occupied the room or building. If only a portion of the building is occupied, it is important to know who else occupies the building, especially those in adjoining spaces. If there are others who operate within the building, anyone having recently moved in should be carefully scrutinized, especially if they have moved into an adjoining space.

When searching for electronic eavesdropping devices, the investigator should not be misled by devices that may have been left as decoys, bugs intended to lead the investigator into thinking that he has found and disposed of the threat. All lines and wires leading into and about the building should be scrutinized. A volt-ohm meter is necessary for this purpose. It is important that the lines be examined and verified to be what they purport to be. In addition to the volt-ohm meter, an array of sophisticated aids to locating hidden microphones, radio transmitters, and telephone taps is also available. Technology is constantly improving such equipment, and the various manufacturers/distributors should be contacted for their literature.

It was mentioned earlier that an eavesdropper will at times alter the wiring within a telephone so that the microphone will become alive and pick up all sounds within its range. To determine if a telephone has undergone such an alteration, the investigator must simply remove the mouthpiece and check with a volt-ohm meter to determine if there is a current passing through the transmitter microphone contacts while the telephone switch is in the hang-up position. If there is, the telephone has been tampered with, and the telephone company should be notified.

The investigator, when searching for eavesdropping devices, should be aware of the existence of contact microphones, also known as vibration microphones. Such microphones often feature either a spike or a suction cup, which is placed in contact with a surface whose vibrations will be picked up by the microphone. These devices are used by the eavesdropper to listen through window panes, by placing the microphone against the glass, and through walls, by sitting in an adjoining room and sticking the spike of the microphone through a hole in one side of the wall and against the wall of the adjoining room, which acts as a diaphragm for any sounds within. If a person is conducting a conversation in a room and fears the possible presence of such a device, he will do well to place a radio or television set so that its speakers are directed towards the suspect wall or door.

Defeating Eavesdropping Efforts

Because of the time, cost, and uncertainty often associated with detecting and neutralizing eavesdropping devices, the decision is sometimes made always to operate as if a device were present and simply take appropriate measures to render its interceptions unintelligible. That may be done in lieu of searching for the device or as a precautionary measure in case a search has failed to uncover an existing device.

With *protective* rather than *detective* measures, some means by which to *mask* the communications or to conduct the sensitive communications in a specially constructed space from which a radio signal cannot transmit is common. The most appropriate protective measures must be determined by a competent specialist in accordance with existing conditions. In determining whether to attempt to negate the effectiveness of eavesdropping devices, the consequences of certain information falling into the wrong hands must be considered. As with all loss prevention and protective efforts, the cost of implementing safeguards, to be justified, must not outweigh the savings.

Chapter Thirteen

CHECKER OR HONESTY TESTING

HONESTY testing, more often referred to as a *checking service*, is a procedure in which an investigator is engaged to pose as a customer. He uses this pretext so that he may observe employees handling cash or negotiable items to determine whether these employees are following established procedures and policy. This service can be readily adapted to fit virtually any operation in which money is exchanged for goods or services.

Checking services have been performed for a number of years by investigative agencies and are a somewhat specialized area. In the past, they were primarily performed for supermarkets and a limited number of other retail outlets. In more recent times, however, the use of this service has broadened to include virtually all types of establishments wherein goods and services are sold to the general public.

While the investigator is generally engaged by management to observe cash-handling procedures, he should strive to give a complete report on the status of all personnel and procedures with which he comes into contact. For example, his report should include comments regarding the courtesy or lack of courtesy of employees and cleanliness of the area, as well as comments he may have overheard from any employees or customers.

This type of investigation is not of itself very time-consuming, and it is generally advisable for the investigator to perform this service in conjunction with other work, unless he intends to specialize in this field. Most individual checks of an establishment can be performed in between thirty and ninety minutes. The time variance comes from the difference between, for example, making a couple of purchases in a grocery store and going through the checkout counter as opposed to conducting a check in a bar or cocktail lounge, where the investigator would normally spend an hour to an hour and a half observing the bartender and cocktail waitresses.

Some investigators, in reporting on this work, use strictly a narrative style. There is much merit in this, provided that the investigator is capable of writing good reports and regularly performs this service. A well-written, narrative-style report prepared by an investigator who thoroughly knows what he is doing makes an excellent appearance.

For the sake of expediency, checklist reports lend themselves well to this operation. They enable an investigator to conduct a thorough check and spend a minimum amount of time in both training prior to doing the check and preparing his report at the conclusion of the check. The report itself is a reminder to the investigator of all the areas he should be concerned with while performing the operation; it ensures that he makes observations in all the critical areas. It also allows management personnel reviewing the reports to do so rapidly, due to their uniformity. Any checklist report should contain a narrative section at the end so that any discrepancies or derogatory information may be elaborated upon.

For those who desire to market this service, consideration should be given to providing the service for a flat rate plus items purchased during the check, as opposed to charging time, expenses, and purchases. To arrive at a flat rate figure, the investigator should consider the total time used traveling to and from the site of the check plus the time necessary to perform the check, as well as normal transportation charges. These costs should then be incorporated into a flat rate figure. Items purchased during the check should not be included in the flat rate charge, as they may vary considerably. Merchandise purchases would then be added to the flat rate. Items purchased during these checks, except those consumed on the premises, of course, should be returned to the client in a manner that does not alert employees to what has taken place.

Chapter Fourteen

STORE DETECTIVES

GENERAL CONSIDERATIONS

T HE store detective is not always referred to as an investigator. In many instances he is considered a plainclothed security guard. Whether he is a private investigator or a security guard will generally depend upon the licensing ordinances in the area in which he is working. However, the store detective's duties are generally the same regardless of how he is classified for licensing purposes, if he is required to be licensed at all.

A store detective is assigned to a particular store or group of stores where a shoplifting problem is suspected. The store detective's primary job is deterring shoplifters. Some may argue with this by saying a store detective's primary function and responsibility is *apprehending* shoplifters, and this is true in part. The main reason that a store owner or manager will employ a store detective is to cut down on his shoplifting losses; by apprehending shoplifters the store detective is creating a deterrent, because other shoplifters will quickly learn that a particular store is actively pursuing shoplifters. The shoplifting activities in such stores will generally be less than those in a store where there is no such deterrent. Therefore, the store detective is acting as a deterrent. Shoplifting is the taking, without consent, of any article of value from a store, with the intent to deprive that store of its ownership. There are, therefore, two steps involved in the act of shoplifting. First is taking the merchandise, and second is carrying the merchandise away with the intention of stealing it. To obtain a conviction against someone arrested and charged with shoplifting, these two points must be proved. Laws in each city, county, and state may vary somewhat as to the way in which shoplifting is defined and exactly what elements are necessary to constitute this offense.

Anyone acting as a store detective or hiring and detailing store detectives must be thoroughly familiar with the ordinances and statutes in his particular area before ever setting foot into the store. As a general rule, the suspected shoplifter must leave the store with the article he has stolen before the court will accept the argument that a theft has actually been committed. In some areas, concealing the article under the suspect's shirt, handbag, or coat is sufficient to support the contention that the individual intended to steal the article and actually made an effort to execute his intentions, but it is still desirable that the suspected shoplifter not be apprehended until he actually leaves the premises with the article. Even if concealment is sufficient to constitute the offense, it cannot hurt the case for the store detective to testify that the defendant actually left the store with the merchandise. Arresting outside the store makes a strong case because there is little room for doubt that the individual actually intended to take the store's property without paying for it. Again, however, the detective should realize that there are variances in the shoplifting laws from one community to another, and he must know the law thoroughly before going on the job. The various types of shoplifters generally fall into six basic categories:

1. The amateur adult shoplifter
2. The juvenile shoplifter
3. The professional shoplifter
4. The kleptomaniac
5. The shoplifter-addict
6. The vagrant and alcoholic shoplifter

It is extremely important that the store detective look and dress the part. He should not wear a trench coat and dark glasses; rather, a store detective must look as much a part of the store's regular clientele as possible. When working a high-class store, he must dress in a high-class manner. When in a discount store, he should wear casual clothes. In either case, he must not attract attention to himself by his dress.

Once on the job, the investigator should look and act as if he is really shopping. If most of the shoppers are pushing shopping carts, the investigator should do likewise. It is important not to move about too quickly yet not to spend too much time in any one place. Prearranged signals can be worked out with other store personnel, so that if any suspicious activity is observed they can discretely alert the investigator without alerting the entire store. If the store has a public address system, it is desirable to use it. A simple page, such as "Miss Anderson, please come to housewares," can be enough to alert the investigator to the fact that there is a suspected shoplifter working the housewares department. (Better still is a number to designate each department, so that only store personnel will know what department is being referred to.) The investigator should then proceed in a normal manner to the department in question. He should not go dashing away, because professional shoplifters working in teams sometimes have one of their team act suspicious so that they can identify the store detective by the way he rushes to the area.

There are a number of conditions that will alert a store detective to the fact that a shoplifter may be present. Such things as a large group of teenagers entering the store together and then splitting up into smaller groups can mean trouble. Customers wearing clothing heavier than the weather and season justify may be viewed with suspicion. Other suspicious conditions include the following: two or three persons grouped together around a counter and restricting the view of the sales clerks, people folding or crumpling merchandise, two or more customers shuffling articles at the same time and at the same counter, and nervous actions such as perspiring freely or moistening dry lips. A customer that faints, becomes ill, or causes some kind of disturbance could be a diversion while an accomplice is stealing. Further suspicious actions are a customer who is more observant and interested in what is going on around him or her than in the merchandise, a customer examining merchandise in odd locations, and a woman who enters the hat or purse department without a hat or purse. These and many more little, seemingly insignificant details immediately flash a warning to the experienced store detective. Any customer who exhibits one or more of these telltale signs will warrant close observation.

Studies have shown that certain areas in a department store are more frequented by shoplifters than others. They are, in the order of frequency, as follows:

1. Men's furnishings
2. Jewelry
3. Sweaters, skirts, and jackets
4. Active sportswear
5. Women's sportwear
6. Blouses
7. Cosmetics
8. Junior sports apparel
9. Children's wear
10. Dresses

The most critical hours for the store detective are between 3:00 pm and 7:00 pm. The most vulnerable days of the week for shoplifting are in order Saturday, Friday, Thursday, Sunday, Monday, Wednesday, and Tuesday.

TELLTALE CLUES

1. Sometimes hair is rearranged to hide small items.
2. Palming is aided by the use of packages, hankies, and gloves.
3. Double-elastic waistbands form hidden pockets inside skirts and trousers.
4. Professionals often use rubber bands with suction cups or hooks fas-

tened inside a coat or jacket sleeve.

5. Slits form false pockets inside jackets, skirts, and trousers.

6. Umbrellas are good catchalls, especially when hung over the arm and held below counter level.

7. Wide skirts, capes, and overcoats provide good hiding places.

8. A long belt with extra eyelets is often used to strap merchandise to the waist beneath clothing.

9. Knitting bags, brief cases, and newspapers form pouches for small articles.

10. A rubber band around bundles of ties, stockings, and socks is used to hook items beneath outer garments.

11. Clothespin snappers, wire hooks, and loops are fastened under arms or skirts or on round garters on the leg.

12. Hats, gloves, pocketbooks, and scarves are often worn out of the store as the customer's own. Sweaters, too, can be worn out or casually carried out on the arm.

13. Some teams work the fitting room. One generally remains there while the other repeatedly moves to the sales floor, bringing new garments back and forth. In crowded conditions they are able to hide or wear garments under their own clothes.

14. Satchels, boxes, and large purses carried into the fitting room or lavatories are potential hiding places for stolen items.

15. With the hard-to-fit or hard-to-please woman who makes repeated trips to and from the fitting room, if the rooms are not kept clear of surplus garments, it is impossible to keep accurate check on the limited number (usually three) she should have when she leaves.

16. Man-woman teams usually work this way: One serves as a "lookout" while the other, in most cases casually carrying a coat or large bag, lifts merchandise.

17. Counters where customers try on shoes or sweaters in the aisles are often crowded at special sales. Shoplifters use this confusion to wear or carry merchandise out of the store.

18. Entire bolts or piece goods can be stolen with relative ease by slick operators. They use special long-slit pockets built into their coats or skirts, which hold the bolt upright. Some wrap a jacket or sweater around the bolt and carry it on the arm.

19. A woman will sometimes tuck a sweater or blouse inside a jacket, then button it up and walk out.

20. A persistent bell-ringer in a self-service department may be distracting a clerk while an accomplice lifts merchandise.

21. Many articles are carried suspended between the legs. Men and women use garters and rubber bands to fasten stolen items to their calves.

22. In large stores a shoplifter may pick up a dropped or carelessly placed name tag. Using the tag, the thief can move freely into stock areas.

23. Many shoplifters place a coat or jacket on top of the counter over the article they want. It is then a simple matter to pick up the coat and item and walk out.

24. The shopper who wears a coat or jacket over the shoulder warrants watching.

25. Sometimes an accomplice will deliberately get into a long conversation or argument to distract a clerk.

26. The female shopper who has a purse yet carries her billfold separately may be using the purse to stash merchandise.

27. Collusion between employees and customers is a possibility the detective must be alert for.

BEFORE THE APPREHENSION

Before making any apprehension, the store detective must be sure that the following events have taken place:

1. The store detective must have actually witnessed the theft himself. The fact that a clerk tells him a theft has occurred is not sufficient.

2. The store detective must be positive that the merchandise the suspected shoplifter has in his possession is actually the property of his client. Many times a person has taken merchandise similar to that of the client into the store and actually *tried* to be apprehended, so that he could later show that the merchandise was not the client's and file a lawsuit for false arrest.

3. The suspected shoplifter must be kept under constant suveillance from the time he is observed committing the theft until he is intercepted by the store detective. If the suspect has had any opportunity to dispose of the merchandise, he should not be apprehended. To proceed with the apprehension in spite of the fact that the suspect has had opportunity to dispose of the merchandise is to invite a false arrest suit. Shoplifters will often work in pairs. When they operate in this fashion, one generally steals an item and passes it to the other or leaves it where he can pick it up.

4. When actually apprehending a suspected shoplifter, the store detective must know exactly what it is the shoplifter stole and where on his person the merchandise is concealed.

5. The store detective, when he appears in court, will have to convince the court that the suspected shoplifter actually intended. to steal the merchandise. The best way to do this is to make the apprehension outside of

court that the suspected shoplifter actually intended to steal the merchandise. The best way to do this is to make the apprehension outside of the store so that there is no question but that the shoplifter actually intended to steal the merchandise.

THE APPREHENSION

When apprehending a suspected shoplifter, the store detective must refrain from using loud or profane language or treating the shoplifter in less than a dignified manner. The store detective should be reserved in his approach and attempt to keep the shoplifter calm. The first question that the store detective should ask the shoplifter is, "Is this the first time you have ever done this?" The shoplifter will invariably say "yes," which is an admission of guilt.

The store detective should then politely request that the shoplifter accompany him back into the store. If at this point in the apprehension the suspected shoplifter attempts to run away, the store detective should not try to apprehend him. The possibility of someone, including the store detective, being injured, possibly seriously, is too great. Technically, the store detective runs the risk of being charged with assault should he employ force in his attempt to apprehend a shoplifter. The fact that the shoplifter was observed stealing in that store will probably be sufficient to prevent the individual's return and certainly to prevent any future shoplifting attempts by that individual.

If the store detective is successful in persuading the shoplifter to accompany him back into the store, he should take the shoplifter to a secluded location and interrogate him. During the apprehension and interrogation stages, it is very important to have present a witness who will attest to the methods used during the apprehension and interrogation. This is extremely important if the store detective is a man and the suspected shoplifter is a woman. It is not uncommon for a female shoplifter to say that a male store detective molested her in some way. This could easily make the store detective the accused instead of the accuser.

Assuming that everything has gone smoothly up to that point and the store detective is ready to interrogate the suspected shoplifter, he should select an area that is away from customers, where he can be assured that the interrogation will proceed uninterrupted. The store detective should remain calm and somewhat sympathetic. In this way the store detective attempts to gain the confidence and cooperation of the suspect. The object of the interrogation is to obtain a signed admission of guilt in the theft just witnessed, and possibly information concerning previous thefts.

In attempting to obtain a signed confession, the store detective must be sure that he does not intimidate or coerce the suspect. Similarly, he must not promise anything or threaten the suspect in any way. In most areas, because store detectives are not law enforcement officers, they are not required to give the *Miranda* warning before questioning a suspected shoplifter. This is not true in all areas of the country, however, and the store detective must learn what the law is in his area before going on the job. If the detective is in an area that requires him to give the *Miranda* warning, this must be done before any questioning, for any questions asked prior to administering the warning will not be admitted into evidence.

For those who must give the *Miranda* warning, it is as follows:

1. You have the right to remain silent.
2. Any statement you do make may be used against you as evidence.
3. You have the right to the presence of an attorney, if so desired.
4. If you cannot afford an attorney, one will be appointed for you, if you so desire.

After the warning has been read to the suspect, in order to secure a waiver, the following questions should be asked, and an affirmative reply to each question secured: "Do you understand each of these rights I have explained to you?" "With these rights in mind, do you wish to talk to us now?"

If the shoplifter admits to the theft and agrees to sign a statement to that effect, the detective (or other store personnel) must then decide whether to prosecute. If the suspect refuses to sign a statement, he *must* be prosecuted. Not to prosecute exposes the store detective to a false arrest suit. If the shoplifter signs a confession or statement and the decision is made not to prosecute, for whatever reason, the suspect should be requested to sign a form that releases the store detective and the client from a later charge of false arrest.

The decision to prosecute or not to prosecute can hinge on many considerations. Most stores do not prosecute every shoplifter apprehended. If they did, the store detective would be spending all his time in court, which would take him out of the store, where he is needed. Following is a list of some of the reasons and circumstances under which prosecution is recommended:

1. The person has a previous criminal record
2. The person is a vagrant or in need of physical, mental, or welfare assistance
3. The shoplifter is hostile and uncooperative even though the merchandise was found on his person
4. The value of the merchandise taken was high
5. The shoplifter is obviously a professional and intended to sell the stolen merchandise
6. The shoplifter cannot be identified (He may have a serious criminal background and knows it would be found out if he carried any identification.)

PREPARING FOR COURT

Once the decision has been made to prosecute the shoplifter, there are certain steps that must be taken to ensure that the case will stand up in court. Any merchandise taken from the shoplifter's person will be used as evidence. To preserve the evidence, the merchandise should be placed into a bag, which is then sealed, initialed, and labeled with time, date, name of suspect, and any other data that is felt to be pertinent under the particular circumstances. If the shoplifter has any merchandise in his possession at the time of questioning that he admits was stolen previously, it should be placed in another bag and marked accordingly. Obviously, if any items are of a perishable nature, they must be properly refrigerated to preserve them for court.

If the shoplifter admits to having at his residence other merchandise that was stolen previously, a statement should be taken that lists each item separately, and also a separate release form for these items should be signed. The detective should not go to the suspect's residence and attempt to recover the items, as that is a matter for law enforcement officers.

At the time the apprehension is made, the investigator should write a complete narrative-style report of the shoplifter's activities and the steps taken in the apprehension. This report, along with the statements and release forms, should be safeguarded, as it will be necessary when the case goes to court. In court, the investigator will only be permitted to refer to notes taken or made at the time of the incident to refresh his memory, he must be sure that the report is complete. Whenever handling a suspected shoplifter, it is desirable to do so as rapidly as possible. The detective should not unduly delay the processing of the suspect; yet, he should not hurry to the point that something may be overlooked. If the police are called and the suspect is to be prosecuted, the suspect should be turned over to them as soon as they arrive. Also, the police should be called as soon as the decision is made to prosecute. When the suspect is turned over to the police, the detective should obtain from them a receipt to that effect. If the police are the ones who actually draw up the complaint, the store detective should go over their report to ensure that all the facts have been stated correctly.

When it comes time to go to court, it is important that all witnesses receive a subpoena and that they all appear. Cases have been lost because witnesses simply forgot to appear. All who are to testify must realize that their attitudes will affect the opinion and consequently the decision of the court. This being the case, it is important that no prejudice be apparent in their testimony. Only the facts must be attested to, not opinion. If witnesses answer questions as impartial bystanders, without favoring either side, the court is more apt to give their evidence the weight it deserves.

If necessary to concede a point to the defense, the witness should do so gracefully, for an angry witness is likely to prejudice the court against his testimony. Before going on the stand, or even into court, the witness should review the statements and evidence thoroughly so that he can speak factually while on the stand. A witness who is positive about his answers and can speak and answer questions in a positive manner will impress the court and offer the defense attorney less room to attempt to cloud and confuse the issue.

When asked a question on the stand, the witness should answer that question and no other. He should never attempt to elaborate or volunteer information unless requested to do so. If he is unable to answer a question or does not know the answer, he should say so. It is important to think about each question before trying to answer it. If he cannot remember, he should so state; it is not a disgrace. If a question is not understood, he should ask that it be repeated or rephrased. He should not attempt to answer when unsure of the question, for that can only lead to problems.

The prosecution must also, of course, be prepared to prove that the merchandise entered as evidence is owned by the store.

Chapter Fifteen

LAWS REGULATING
THE INVESTIGATOR'S ACTIVITIES

LICENSING

INVESTIGATORS will generally find it necessary to comply with licensing requirements prescribed by various political subdivisions. However, the scope of these requirements is far too broad to be treated in detail within this writing. There is a great deal of variation from one area to another as to who is required to be licensed, what qualifications he must possess, and how much the licensing fee is. It should be noted that licensing is most often conducted on the state level, sometimes on the city level, and occasionally on the county level as well. In some instances an investigator will find that he is required to be licensed by all three bodies. Because of these inconsistent licensing requirements, each investigator will find it necessary to determine what the laws are in each area where he will conduct business. The investigator will do well not to minimize the seriousness of these laws, as penalties for their violation can be severe and may prevent him from further pursuing this field of endeavor.

FAIR CREDIT REPORTING ACT

Public law 91-508, commonly referred to as the *Fair Credit Reporting Act*, while being rather lengthy, simply lays out requirements that must be adhered to when providing or using information pertaining to an applicant's eligibility for —

1. Credit
2. Insurance
3. Employment

The primary purpose of this act is to enable a person who has been denied either credit, insurance, or employment because of information reflected in an investigative report to examine and challenge the validity of such information. The act thus places a responsibility upon those who provide and use such reports.

Any investigator or investigative agency that intends to engage in this type of reporting would be well advised to obtain a copy of public law 91-508 and become familar with its contents.

PUBLIC INFORMATION RECORDS

There appears to be a general trend towards restricting access to records that were previously considered public information. There is little indication that this trend will be reversed, and the investigator can anticipate a greater need as time goes on to cultivate informants with access to such information.

USE OF BUMPER BEEPER SYSTEMS

The reader should be aware that there have been several important federal court decisions regarding the use of bumper beepers. It is now necessary to obtain a warrant for the use of a beeper if the owner of the vehicle has not consented to its placement upon his vehicle. Recent court decisions provide that a person is protected against unreasonable searches under the Fourth Amendment and has a right to expect that his property (his vehicle, in this case) is free from the trespass necessary to install a beeper. This right of privacy, according to the recent court decisions, extends to freedom to travel about without unreasonable government monitoring.

In *United States v. Martyniuk*, the court found that in installing a beeper, investigators were "looking for" evidence and instrumentalities of crime that would incriminate the person in possession of the property to which the beeper was attached. For this reason, the placement of a beeper constituted a search under the Fourth Amendment. The court also found that the placement of the beeper was in violation of the subject's right to privacy, as it served to monitor his movements and location, both of which may legitimately be private.

What the recent decisions essentially mean is that if a client desires to have, for example, his delivery trucks surveilled and consents to the placement of a beeper on a vehicle owned or controlled by him, it is perfectly proper for the investigator to engage in such activity. If, however, the owner of the vehicle does not know about the beeper and has not consented to its placement, the act is not legal unless the proper warrant is first obtained.

The reader may wish to refer to *United States v. Martyniuk*, 395 F. Supp. 42 (May 19, 1975) or *United States v. Holmes*, No. 74-2419 (October 8, 1975).

Chapter Sixteen

GENERAL CONCLUSIONS

IT is the authors' hope that this writing has proven beneficial as a learning aid for aspiring young investigators and as a refresher for those investigators with a considerable degree of experience, and that it will be a reference source that can be referred to by all investigators on a daily basis when conducting live investigations.

The authors have endeavored to identify and illustrate the field of private investigation as a whole and the kind of individual most likely to succeed at this calling and, at the same time, to dispel the many myths concerning this field, not the least of which is the glamour depicted by fiction.

For those readers not actually engaged in investigative work, this book should have provided an understanding of the rudiments of this profession. Quite simply, private investigators are individuals who gather various types of information for various reasons, taking effective notes while information is being gathered and finally preparing an informative report reflecting their findings.

An attempt has been made to illustrate the differences between the criminal investigative agencies (law enforcement investigations) and private investigative agencies and, while so doing, to dispel the belief that law enforcement investigators are in competition with non-law enforcement investigators. The reader should understand that these are two distinctly different callings geared for the fulfillment of two very different needs and that, therefore, many of these techniques and methods, while similar in some respects, possess a number of differences in both the reasons for and the manner in which they are applied.

Finally, it is the authors' sincere desire that law enforcement investigators also will have found that this writing has broadened their knowledge and thus enhanced their versatility as investigators. As stated, governmental and private investigators operate in generally different ways, but experience has shown that governmental investigators frequently encounter situations in which they would do well to consider a technique or method that is more commonly employed by private investigators. The extent to which governmental investigators can employ the techniques characteristic of private investigators is controlled to a large degree by laws regarding search and seizure, but where such restrictions do not exist, governmental investigators are encouraged to at least consider the potential of these methods. This is especially true for pretext investigations.

GLOSSARY OF TERMS CHARACTERISTIC OF THE LEGAL AND INVESTIGATIVE PROFESSIONS

THE investigative profession, just like any other trade or profession, uses certain characteristic words. The following list of words is not all-inclusive, but it does contain some of the more commonly used words that the investigator should be aware of and understand.

Abstract of Title. ·A statement of the conveyance by which successive owners have acquired title to real estate

Affidavit. A statement, in writing, sworn to before a person authorized by law to take oaths; it is made without cross-examination and in this respect differs from a deposition

Allegation. The statement of a person in court concerning the things he intends to prove

Apprehend. To effect an arrest, or take into custody, a person suspected of having committed a crime

Arraign. To bring a prisoner before the court, read the indictment to the prisoner, and have the prisoner plead guilty or not guilty

Assumpsit. An action to recover damages for a breach or nonperformance of a contract or promise, oral or written

Bankrupt. Insolvent, unable to pay any debts. The Bankruptcy Act is a federal statute providing for the distribution of the assets of a bankrupt to specified creditors. A voluntary petition in bankruptcy is one filed by a person, persons, firm, or corporation seeking relief from debts. An involuntary petition in bankruptcy is filed by a group of creditors against a person, firm, or corporation believed involved to the extent of being bankrupt.

Chattel Mortgage. A mortgage on personal property, as distinguished from one on real property

Claimant. Person who files a claim against an insurance company

Composition. An agreement among creditors and with their debtor whereby each creditor is to be paid less than the amount of his claim

Contingent Liability. An amount resulting from past transactions that may become a liability in the future under certain defined circumstances

Contributory negligence. The lack of ordinary care on the part of an injured person to such an extent that he cannot recover damages, although another person's negligence is involved

Conveyance. An instrument used to transfer title to real property; transfer of title to real property to another

Cover. Anything that can be used to help conceal a person's presence or activities. When used in connection with a physical surveillance, *cover* is anything that is between the investigator and the subject and allows the investigator to observe his subject without being seen by the subject. The term *cover* is also applied to a story or pretext that an investigator may use to substantiate his being in a particular place.

Defendant. A person required to make answer in an action or suit of law or equity or in a criminal action

Deficiency Judgment. A judgment for the balance of a debt after the security has been realized and the proceeds applied to payment; especially such a judgment following foreclosure of a mortgage

Demurrer. A pleading that admits the facts but denies that they have legal effect

Discharge of Bankruptcy. An order that terminates bankruptcy proceedings, usually relieving the debtor of all legal responsibility for certain specified obligations

Encumbrance. A lien or liability attached to real property

Ex Parte. Ordinarily implies a hearing or examination in the presence of, or on papers filed by, one party and in the absence of, and often without notice to, the other party

Forcible Entry and Detainer. The statutory proceeding to regain possession of land or a tenement by force

Grantee. One to whom a grant is made

Granter. One who grants credit

Grantor. The person by whom a grant is made

Habeas Corpus. A writ directing one who has custody of another to bring him before the court to determine the right to hold such person in custody

Indemnity. That which is given as compensation for loss

Informant. A term that refers to a person who supplies information to an investigator. An *informant* is usually an *unbiased* source of information, who may be supplying information simply because he wishes to help the investigator or who may be doing so for a fee.

Informer. A person who supplies information to an investigator, usually because of some personal reason. Many times an *informer* is himself a criminal, and he supplies the information in the hope that a person whom he personally dislikes may be prosecuted. An *informer* is a person for whom most people have little respect.

Injunction. An order of a court of equity directing a person to do or refrain from doing some act

Interrogation. The act of questioning a person who is believed to have committed a particular action. The objective of an *interrogation* is generally to obtain a confession from the person being questioned

Interview. The act of questioning an individual who may be in possession of information the questioner is in search of

Intestate. A person who dies without making a will; not disposed of by will

Joint tenancy. An estate held by two or more persons in which the interest of anyone dying passes to the surviving tenant

Lien. A charge upon real or personal property for the satisfaction of some debt or duty until some claim is paid or satisfied

Misdemeanor. A minor crime punishable by fine or jail sentence or both

Physical Surveillance. The act of observing a person or place to gain information. The person making the observations is often referred to as the *surveillant,* while the person being watched is called the *subject. Physical surveillance* operations are usually referred to by investigators as simply *surveillance. Surveillance* conducted at one location is generally referred to as *stationary surveillance* but sometimes is called *fixed surveillance* or a *stake-out. Surveillance* conducted on a subject traveling from one location to another, either on foot or by some type of conveyance, is referred to as *moving surveillance.*

Plaintiff. One who commences a suit to obtain a remedy for an injury to his rights

Power of Attorney. A written instrument appointing an agent and giving him power to contract for his principal

Pretext. An investigative method used to obtain the cooperation of people under circumstances that would result in resistance and refusal were the investigator's true identity and purpose known. When using a pretext, the investigator simply makes up a fictitious reason, supported by props, for asking certain questions and/or entering certain areas.

Quitclaim Deed. A deed that conveys whatever interest the grantor may have in a property

Replevin. The writ by which, or the action in which, personal property wrongfully taken is returned to the rightful owner

Roping. The act of using a pretext to gain information; occurs when an investigator desires certain information from a particular person and obtains it without asking any direct questions

Statute of Limitations. A statute assigning a certain time after which rights cannot be enforced by action

Subrogation. To substitute one person for another as a creditor

Sub Rosa. The act of questioning a claimant, his neighbors, or relatives utilizing a pretext. Insurance claims adjustors also refer to this type of activity as *undercover* work. *Sub rosa* is a term most generally used by or in connection with insurance people and refers to the same type of operation as do the terms *pretext* and *roping.*

Suit. An action or process in a court for the recovery of a right or claim

Summons. A written order commanding a defendant to appear in court and answer to the charge of the plaintiff

Testator. A person who leaves a will in force at his death

Tort. A wrong arising independently of a contract; a private wrong as distinguished from a crime

Trust. A property interest held by one person for the benefit of another

Trust Deed. A deed that conveys real property to a second person to be held in trust for the benefit of a third person

Trustee. A person who has legal title to property, the income of which goes to another person

Undercover. From a police or industrial standpoint, this word tends to denote a long-term operation whereby an investigator goes undercover into a factory or warehouse, for example, to gain the confidence of the people working in that area, using this confidence to obtain the desired information. This type of an operation may run for several days to several months. When talking with insurance claims adjustors, however, the word *undercover* has a different meaning (*see sub rosa*).

Vendee. One who buys

Vendor. One who sells

Venue. The place or county where a suit is brought

Waive. To surrender, abandon, or relinquish a right

Writ. An order of a court commanding that the will of the court be obeyed

Appendix B

SOCIAL SECURITY NUMBERS:
STATES OF ORIGIN

T HE first three digits of a social security number reflect the state or territory in which the number was issued, except for the series 700 through 729,
which is a separate series of numbers issued only to retired railroad employees.

001-003	New Hampshire	387-399	Wisconsin
004-007	Maine	400-407	Kentucky
008-009	Vermont	408-415	Tennessee
010-034	Massachusetts	416-424	Alabama
035-039	Rhode Island	425-428, 587	Mississippi
040-049	Connecticut	429-432	Arkansas
050-134	New York	433-439	Louisiana
135-158	New Jersey	440-448	Oklahoma
159-211	Pennsylvania	449-467	Texas
212-220	Maryland	468-477	Minnesota
221-222	Delaware	478-485	Iowa
223-231	Virginia	486-500	Missouri
232-236	West Virginia	501-502	North Dakota
237-246	North Carolina	503-504	South Dakota
247-251	South Carolina	505-508	Nebraska
252-260	Georgia	509-515	Kansas
261-267	Florida	516-517	Montana
268-302	Ohio	518-519	Idaho
303-317	Indiana	520	Wyoming
318-361	Illinois	521-524	Colorado
362-386	Michigan	525, 585	New Mexico

526-527	Arizona	575-576	Hawaii
528-529	Utah	577-579	District of Columbia
530	Nevada	580	Virgin Islands
531-539	Washington	581-584	Puerto Rico
540-544	Oregon	586	Guam
545-573	California	586	American Samoa
574	Alaska	700-729	Railroad retirement

COMMON ERRORS IN LICENSE NUMBERS

WITNESSES will occasionally make errors when observing a license number or when reporting the number to someone verbally. Certain errors in the observation or reporting of numerals and digits occur more frequently than others. Because certain numbers and letters are easily mistaken in appearance or sound with others, the following listing should be of assistance to investigators when a witness reports a vehicle license number but there is apparently an error.

COMMON ERRORS BY OBSERVATION

A for H	R for F-H-K-P
B for D-E-S-H-8	S for B-8
C for G-O-Q	T for E-F-P
D for O-Q-P-U	U for D-J-O-Q
E for F-H-K-P-R-T	V for M-N-U-W-X-Y
F for E-H-K-P-R-T	W for M-N-V-X-Y
G for C-O-Q	X for K-V-Y
H for E-R-K-R-N-B	Y for K-V-X
J for O-Q-U	Z for E-K-S-X
K for E-F-H-N-P-R-Y	1 for 7
L for E-T	2 for 5-7
M for N-V-W-X	3 for 5-6-8
N for H-M-V-W-X	4 for 1
O for C-D-G-Q-U	5 for 2-3
P for F-R-T	6 for 0-8
Q for C-D-G-O-U	7 for 1-2

8 for 3-6-9   9 for 0-8

COMMON ERRORS BY SOUND

A for H-J-K   N for F-M

B for C-D-E-G-P-T-V-Z   P for B-C-D-E-G-T-V-Z

C for B-D-E-G-P-T-V-Z   Q for U

D for B-C-E-G-P-T-V-Z   S for F-N-X

E for B-C-D-G-P-T-V-Z   T for B-C-D-E-G-P-V-Z

F for N-X-S   U for Q

G for B-C-D-E-P-T-V-Z   V for B-C-D-E-G-P-T-Z

H for A-J-K   X for F-S

J for A-H-K   Y for I

K for A-H-J   Z for B-C-D-E-G-P-T-V

M for F-N

INDEX